ELECTRONICS RESOURCES RESOURCES MANAGEMENT IN THE ACADEMIC LIBRARY

ELECTRONICS RESOURCES RESOURCES MANAGEMENT IN THE ACADEMIC LIBRARY

A Professional Guide

Karin Wikoff

 LIBRARIES UNLIMITED

AN IMPRINT OF ABC-CLIO, LLC
Santa Barbara, California • Denver, Colorado • Oxford, England

Copyright 2012 by Karin Wikoff

All rights reserved. No part of this publication may be reproduced, stored in a retrieval
system, or transmitted, in any form or by any means, electronic, mechanical,
photocopying, recording, or otherwise, except for the inclusion of brief quotations in a
review or reproducibles, which may be copied for classroom and educational programs
only, without prior permission in writing from the publisher.

Library of Congress Cataloging-in-Publication Data

Wikoff, Karin.
    Electronics resources management in the academic library : a professional guide / Karin Wikoff.
        p. cm.
    Includes bibliographical references and index.
    ISBN 978–1–61069–005–8 (pbk. : acid-free paper) — ISBN 978–1–61069–006–5 (ebook)
1. Libraries—Special collections—Electronic information resources. 2. Electronic information
resources—Management. 3. Academic libraries—Collection development. 4. Libraries and
electronic publishing. I. Title.
Z692.C65W55   2012
025.17′4—dc23   2011035284

ISBN: 978–1–61069–005–8
EISBN: 978–1–61069–006–5

16 15 14 13 12   1 2 3 4 5

This book is also available on the World Wide Web as an eBook.
Visit www.abc-clio.com for details.

Libraries Unlimited
An Imprint of ABC-CLIO, LLC

ABC-CLIO, LLC
130 Cremona Drive, P.O. Box 1911
Santa Barbara, California 93116-1911

This book is printed on acid-free paper ∞

Manufactured in the United States of America

Contents

Preface

Licensed electronic resources have become the cornerstone of academic research, making their management mission-critical for college and university libraries. However, shockingly few library schools offer instruction in e-resource management. Many times the management of these resources falls to someone who has to scramble to figure it out on the fly.

This book covers the whole life cycle of electronic resources, from acquiring through providing access to administering, supporting, and evaluating. Specific issues include vendor relations, negotiating contracts, access models, troubleshooting, gathering and using statistics, collection development, linking technologies, and much more. After working through this book, you should have a grasp of the issues you would face as an electronic resources librarian along with some practical working knowledge to get you started in this exciting and fast-paced field.

Each of the main chapters covers one of the five life-cycle points. At the end of each chapter, there are suggested readings, thought-provoking questions to think through and discuss with colleagues, and assignments that require interaction with real-world situations. The benefit of the assignments is in the process; there are no right or wrong answers.

For each chapter, you should apply the following work flow:

First, read the chapter and any accompanying materials in the Appendixes.

Then, read at least two of the articles in the Selected Readings and answer the questions in the Thought Provokers section. If you can find friends or colleagues with whom to discuss these questions, you'll be giving yourself added benefits of their experience and perspectives. If you are using this book in a formal course, you'll be able to have discussions with your classmates.

The current article assignments are third. These are designed to make sure that you are examining new and up-to-date issues related to electronic resources. If you are not currently at an institution that has access to commercial academic databases, it may take a little more work, but there are freely available journals and articles on the Internet (Try Library Journal at http://www.libraryjournal.com), or you might try walking into a local academic library and reading materials on the premises.

Then do the assignment for the chapter. Several of these require you to contact either a vendor sales representative or someone currently employed in a library or academic ITS department. A vendor's website should have a means of contacting a salesperson, and you will find that most of them are more than happy to talk with you about their products. Whether you are a current student or an independent learner, you are a potential future customer, and they will want to establish a positive view of their company and its products. As for librarians and other information professionals, unless you are already working in a library, you may have to make a few calls, but on the whole, librarians are friendly people interested in furthering our profession, and they should be willing to work with you.

If you are a library school instructor, you can facilitate these assignments by contacting a few vendors and colleagues ahead of time, making sure they are willing to help. You can also send them the relevant assignment(s) as a heads-up. If you like, you can assign students to specific vendors to be sure you get an even spread, and you can provide your students with the contact information as well.

Finally, there is the capstone assignment. Instructors may want to make this a small group project. You are asked to write your own electronic resources collection development document. You will draw on everything you learn in the course of reading the book and doing the assignments. You can work on this assignment as you go, or you can save it until the end, but you will want to complete the book before you complete this assignment to make sure you have all of the most pertinent information to guide you in writing your document. When it is done, you have something tangible to show for all your efforts, something which may be useful at the institution where you work or something which you could put on a resume.

Let's have a look at the layout of the book.

Chapter One covers the definition of electronic resources. This is a moving target not only because new models seem to be appearing daily, but also because the definitions will vary from institution to institution according to what resources they expect their e-resource manager to manage. Nonetheless, it is useful to start with some basic definitions and then adjust according to the environment in which you find yourself. In particular, we look at various kinds of databases, e-journals and e-journal collections, e-books and e-book collections, hybrid combinations of all of the above, and a few linking technologies, such as Open URL and Z39.50. You get a break; there are no selected readings or current article assignments with Chapter One.

Chapter Two is all about the acquisition of e-resources. We start with the collection development document as the guide to selecting the e-resources you want to acquire. We then discuss comparison shopping and how to find the best deal, and finally we have a look at the process of ordering and paying.

Chapter Three has details on how to set up and provide access to the e-resources you manage. It's a lot to cover here from IP addresses to proxy servers to OPACS. It also covers a wide range of different kinds of portals and holdings management services. We look at the particulars for e-journals and e-books, and have a quick peek at usability testing, which is covered in another chapter in more detail. Perhaps the most important part of the chapter is the importance of your relations with whatever information technology services you have at your institution.

Chapter Four is on the administration of e-resources. We spend a fair amount of time on licenses, including SERU, and then look closely at all the various places where information about e-resources is stored and administered. From bulk-loading MARC records into your OPAC, to "hooking" acquisitions data from your ILS into an ERM, to overlap analysis and other functionality in holdings management services, to not overlooking information sources such as e-mail files and human memory. We wrap up with a first look at the URMs of the future.

Chapter Five addresses the troubleshooting of e-resources. We cover some basics in the process of elimination for diagnosing the source of problems, consider where to turn for help and support in solving problems, and finish with some instructive examples. Problem logs for more efficient tracking of problems are also discussed.

Chapter Six is about the evaluation of e-resources. We look at trials and evaluations, including evaluation tools, and applying collection development criteria both for acquiring and for deselecting resources. Usage statistics and their applications are covered, as are standards such as COUNTER and SUSHI. Then we turn to user feedback, including both surveys and usability studies, and we even take a quick look at the trend of anthropologists helping libraries improve their services.

Chapter Seven is simply the description of the capstone assignment and hence is very brief.

Chapter Eight provides a description of a "typical" day in the life of an electronic resources librarian. All the events of the day are taken from real life and most of them occurred on one day in the spring of 2011.

Chapter Nine provides practical job-hunting tips for those who have worked their way through this book and are beginning to seek a position in the field.

This book is not intended to be exhaustive, but rather to be readable and accessible, the sort of book a self-starter will be more likely to finish reading than a deadly dry and boring textbook, yet it will give you the basics you need to get a good start in a position as an electronic resources manager.

Notes for Library School Instructors

Learning should be an active partnership between the teacher and the students. Your feedback on assignments is invaluable, particularly since the assignments will seldom have "wrong" answers unless the student misunderstood the question. Grading assignments in this class is particularly subjective. You may wish to give full marks for each unless it is obvious the student is way off base or has clearly not put in much effort. In the former case, you may wish to allow the student to resubmit a corrected assignment.

Many students in library school are of nontraditional age, coming from varied backgrounds and often with rich experiences in a wide range of library settings. Be open to letting the learning flow in the other direction as well, from the students to the instructor. The sharing of experiences from different libraries and from different points of view should be encouraged. The instructor should be engaged in the discussions, but should take care not to dominate the conversation or impose his or her personal opinions. Set an example for allowing room to "agree to disagree" respectfully, and you will create an environment in which everyone can benefit from the open exchange of ideas.

While the discussion portion of the course is where the philosophical and theoretical aspects of the topics can be covered; the assignments are designed to provide very practical, hands-on experience working with real-life vendors, librarians, and other professionals with whom an electronic resources librarian would interact on the job. You can facilitate the assignments by contacting a few vendors and colleagues ahead of time, making sure they are willing to help. You can also send them the relevant assignment(s) as a heads-up. If you like, you can assign students to specific vendors to be sure you get an even spread, and you can provide your students with the contact information as well.

The capstone assignment is best used as a group project, such as your students will encounter on the job. Two to four students per group is recommended, as is a mid-semester progress report to be sure no one is leaving the work on what is meant to be a term-long project to the end of the class. You might ask each group to provide you with a list of other collection development policies they have consulted and give you a rough outline of what they plan to cover and how they plan to organize their document. Allow lots of room for different approaches so long as all the essential components are included.

When this course has been taught before, Chapter One was a one-week unit, while Chapters Two through Six were allowed two weeks each. Additional weeks were spent on "hot topics" of the times, with the extra time at the end of the course given to allow students to complete the group project. Chapters Eight and Nine are primarily for the reader's use, although you may integrate the material into your discussions if you wish. You will find a sample syllabus in Appendix K, but you may structure the course any way that suits your purpose.

1

Defining Electronic Resources, or, What Is This Book About, Anyway?

The electronic resources covered in this textbook will include databases, e-journals and e-journal collections, e-books, and some mention of linking technologies and e-resource management systems.

DATABASES

Let's start with the generic term: database. Generally speaking, a card catalog was a database, each card containing a record with certain kinds of information, organized for retrieval. Moving into the world of online public-access catalogs, these records hold similar information but they make it easier and faster to locate books and other library resources. When we are discussing electronic resources in libraries, we are usually talking about commercial databases of academic resources. Here are a few types of these databases:

A&I (Abstracts and Indexing) or Bibliographic Databases: These are databases of citations to articles. Often A&I databases have links to the full-text of the articles referenced, but not always. Some examples of A&I databases include Readers Guide Retrospective from H. W. Wilson, Historical Abstracts, or International Index to Music Periodicals.

Full-Text Databases: For the purposes of categorizing, we'll use the term "full-text" loosely, although perhaps not as loosely as many vendors do. A full-text database not only has an index to articles, but it also provides the full text of most of those articles. Databases which contain the actual object the user is seeking, whether the object is text, image, sound file, statistical data, or some other format information, belong in this category too. InfoTrac Custom Newspapers is a full-text text database; ArtSTOR is a full-text image database; Historical Statistics of the United States is a database of historical quantitative information, that is, full-text statistics.

The tricky part about full-text is how the vendors define it. You would think that *full*-text means everything is there; but it doesn't. Many databases have mostly full-text, but they also include indexing-only for some titles. Sometimes full-text really means that the full-text of everything that appears in every issue of a print equivalent is indeed contained in the database. Sometimes. But more often there will be bits missing: a special issue isn't included or you'll be missing three articles from a particular volume. Other times the text is there, but images that appeared in print are not available in the online version. This has to do with copyright and licensing. It all depends on the contract the author or artist has with the publisher as well as the contract the publisher has with the aggregator or vendor. If the publisher or vendor couldn't get permission to use an article or an image in their online database, those items will be missing. Some vendors set a threshold; for example, perhaps there has to be 75 percent of the original before they call something full-text, but they don't usually advertise this amount, and you never know about it until you run up against a gap, an article you *know* is in print, but it isn't available in the electronic version online. So, be careful how you interpret "full-text" and figure that it is seldom truly fully full-text even when that's what it's called.

Journal Collections: The distinction between a "database" and a "journal collection" is quite fine and totally unnoticed by the majority of our patrons. An aggregated database has a collection of journals that are changeable and unstable. There is little guarantee that content is complete full-text and even less guarantee that what you see there today will still be there tomorrow. Titles come and go from aggregated databases all the time, which is why we have companies like Serials Solutions or TDNet to help us keep track of what we can access in our databases at any given time. A journal collection is generally much more stable and tends to include a more complete full-text. Project MUSE is an example of a current journal collection, while JSTOR is primarily a complementary backfile journal collection. Sage also offers a number of subject area-specific journal collections. Project MUSE and JSTOR have a reputation for being extremely reliable in terms of the titles in their collections. The contracts they have with the publishers are relatively solid, and, on the very rare occasions when a title has dropped out of MUSE, for example, the handful of titles Duke University pulled a few years ago, they could pull out only future issues while the issues already in the collection remain permanently.

Databases and journal collections are searched the same way by users, who expect the same results. They expect to find a full-text article. It won't matter to them if the article comes from a "database" or a "journal collection." The difference to you as the manager of these resources is that the journal collection will probably have fewer titles for a similar price, but the title list will be much more stable. You get more bang for the buck with an aggregated database, but you will get more stability with a journal collection. Most libraries' electronic resource collections will have some of each.

Specialized and Hybrid Databases: In addition to the databases of journal articles, images, and statistical information, you will also run across databases of specialized kinds of information such as the chemical information found in SciFinder Scholar or the drug and herbal remedy overviews in Health and Wellness Resource Center. Other examples include geographic information in Columbia Earthscape, CQ Researcher's research reports, ICSD's crystal structure data, curricular materials for teachers in KCDLOnline, financial analyses in Business and Company Resource Center or Morningstar, compilations of public opinion surveys in Polling the Nations, Arbitron ratings and rankings for radio and records in R&R, sports marketing information in SBRNet, stock information in Value Line, or the product and company register Thomasnet.

Many of these more specialized databases might be called "hybrids;" that is, they contain a mix of things like some articles, some book chapters, some financial reports, some encyclopedia entries, and so forth. You may want to have a few of these resources in your collection to meet the more specific needs of your user population. Business Source Premier is an example of a hybrid database with articles, bibliographies, company reports, SWOT analyses, editorials, obituaries, product reviews, speeches, working papers, and more.

Primary Source Databases: A subset of full-text databases, primary source databases, contain primary source data such as letters, diaries, memoirs, oral histories, and other such materials. Alexander Street Press offers quite a few primary source databases, such as American Civil War Letters and Diaries and Early Encounters in North America. The American Memory project from the Library of Congress is also a primary source database, although it is free and publicly available on the Internet.

E-JOURNALS

The next category of electronic resources is e-journals. As you can see, the categories are already bleeding into one another, which is the norm with electronic resources. To be clear, an e-journal is the electronic version of a print journal or serial publication, although increasingly you can also find journals that are entirely "born digital" and never existed in a print version. You can get access to e-journals through aggregated databases or through journal collections, but you can also purchase individual subscriptions, just like print journals.

As with print journals, you can purchase subscriptions to e-journals directly from the publisher or through a vendor. Major players in this arena are EBSCO, Harrassowitz, and Blackwell's, but there are others, including publishers who sell their own titles as well as the titles from other publishers, which further blurrs distinctions. Occasionally you can find free online e-journals.

Embargo: An embargo is when the publisher delays the most current issues of a title. For example, the Monthly Journal of X may have a six-month embargo, meaning the most recent issue available is six monthly issues back. But if your institution pays for a subscription to the Monthly Journal of X, you will have access to the most recent issue published anywhere. Unlike titles in aggregated databases, a direct e-journal subscription should not be embargoed. Aside from the access issues, which are similar to access issues for databases, managing e-journals is much like managing print serials.

E-BOOKS

E-Books versus Digitized Books: Let's start by differentiating electronic books from digitized books. A digitized book is a print book that has been scanned and saved as a sort of photographic image of the book. An electronic book is generally fully searchable text in a feature-rich environment; it often requires special "reader" software.

Collections: E-books can come as part of a collection, usually broadly themed, such as Social and Behavioral Sciences or Academic Complete from ebrary. These particular collections offer unlimited simultaneous users and readers that are packed with functionality. ebrary collections also allow the users seamless access to individually purchased titles through the same interface. An e-book collection can be static, such as Oxford Reference Online, which has a set list of titles, or it can be updated with new titles being added and old titles removed, some due to obsolescence, and some because publisher agreements change, making e-book collections very similar to aggregated databases.

Custom Packages: E-books can also come in custom packages, with a certain number of titles (or "slots," where a book that would have been thick and cost more had it been printed counts as two "slots," while a thin book with a lower print list price might only count as half a slot) for one price, such as ProQuest's Safari Tech Books Online. This product allows the customer to swap out unused titles for different titles as frequently as once a month.

Individual Titles: E-books can also be purchased one at a time, making their purchase similar to that of regular print books. The important difference is that you will find that your "purchase" is of a perpetual license and does not come with the same privileges librarians are used to having with the purchase of physical books. For example, Fair Use is often more restricted and defined for e-books, while First Sale privileges (which are what allow libraries to lend books under copyright laws) are usually specifically prohibited.

The e-book market is changing rapidly. Publishers, vendors, and aggregators are throwing all kinds of new purchase models out there to see what will work and to make sure they get a healthy share of the market. As a manager of e-books, a person has to be prepared to deal with all kinds of rapidly appearing, never-before-seen models until the market sorts itself out and we see which models work and endure and which ones, like the 8-track, disappear. Meanwhile, there are many options from which to choose. You can buy e-books directly from publishers; you can buy them from aggregators, such as NetLibrary; you can buy them through a regular print book jobber, such as YBP, and have the access delivered through an aggregator platform such as ebrary. You can purchase the content and have your own local platform for delivery (although I doubt many librarians choose that route). You can even purchase a subscription to access an e-book, or you can purchase a perpetual license. You can purchase single-user rights or multiple-user rights. You can set up a deposit account and try Patron Driven Acquisition (PDA) of e-books where the vendor loads records for large collections of e-books into your OPAC, and your institution automatically pays for keeping those that are accessed by patrons more than a certain number of times. You can rent e-books, although this seems an impractical model for libraries. Each option will be priced differently, delivered differently, and carried across time differently, so you need to take care in choosing your options.

Some librarians, mostly public librarians but not exclusively, are making the foray into downloadable e-books that then have to be loaded onto an e-reader and lent as such. The logistics for this kind of content delivery in a library are still rather complicated although there are new developments every week or so; this may become more feasible in the near future.

Free Online E-Books: Just as there are free e-journals on the Internet, there are also free e-books available online. These are of many different types—anything from simple scanned images of books to books set up as complex, searchable relational databases with downloadable spreadsheet data and more. You may find it is part of your job to decide which of these resources you would define as an "e-book" and whether or not you want to include them in your collection.

Reader Software: One of the challenges of e-books can be the accompanying reader software. Some e-books can be read simply in a browser, but most of those in collections or custom packages come with many rich features that require the use of special helper software. This software has to be downloaded, installed, and configured to work on the individual user's system Sometimes it works like a charm; downloading and installing ebrary's original reader over a high bandwidth network to a PC running the latest version of Internet Explorer (IE) was a click and done so fast you hardly noticed. When it first came out, if you tried to download and install it on a Power Mac, you had to go through complicated workarounds, use only certain browsers, change permission settings, and more. If you were trying to download and install it at home on a slow dial-up connection, it would time out and never load any book.

If you didn't have the correct version of Java running on your machine, it wouldn't work. With each new release of the reader software, problems were corrected, but there are trade-offs for all that wonderful functionality in terms of adding a whole additional layer where things can go wrong Some e-book vendors have shifted to browser-based readers that require no downloading and installing. These readers have had less functionality than the downloaded variety, but vendors are working to bring them up to speed so that soon there won't be any appreciable difference.

Hybrids: Quite often when a publisher decides to deliver the content of a print work electronically via the Internet, what was once a "book" becomes something more. Obviously, it becomes searchable, but what if the original print work had tables of data? Why not make those downloadable Excel files? Why not add functionality that wasn't possible in print? Perhaps they not only add working links to related materials, but maybe there's an interactive section or even a discussion forum. The next thing you know it's not really a "book" any more at all, although it still has the same title. You may have a selector come to you to "purchase the online version" of this reference book or print serial, and it turns out to be a "database" or even a "service."

E-Textbooks: In a recent discussion, a librarian from another institution insisted on making a distinction between e-books and e-textbooks. In addition to the distinction between books and textbooks with which we are already familiar, he made a case for an e-textbook having all the hybrid bells and whistles mentioned above. While one may not agree completely with this strict definition, the whole area of e-textbooks is intriguing. It's a developing area that will be worth watching in the next year or two. One hears of e-textbook rental deals where students rent their textbooks for less than it would cost to purchase a hard copy. The student saves some money at the time of purchase, but there would be no more textbook buy-back at the end of the semester, nor any opportunity to sell the book to another student for next year. Additionally, some of these deals are done on a "pay per read" basis. The e-textbook has built-in reporting software that charges the account every time a page is accessed, thereby preventing students from sharing one e-textbook to save money. These new and evolving models for e-book/e-textbook delivery raise a lot of issues librarians will want to follow, whether we choose to ever get into the business of providing our patrons with textbooks or not.

LINKING TECHNOLOGIES

Broadly speaking, linking technologies are standards that allow disparate systems to talk to each other and share information. To the user, linking technologies means not having to manually redo the same search in multiple databases.

In theory, standards are supposed to make things interchangeable. But in reality, the same standard can be implemented entirely differently in one system than it is in another. So, if the standard says that author information should be formatted as `&Author=Smith;` and the title should be formatted as `&Title=Hello World;` and both systems use that standard, things ought to be fine.

If the standard fails to indicate in which order those elements are to be sent, and System A sends `&Author=Smith;&Title=Hello World;` but System B is expecting `&Title=Hello World;&Author=Smith;` the system at the other end *may* be able to sort it out, or it may send all results with Smith in the title, or the search may just fail and you'll be left scratching your head wondering why it didn't work as expected when both parties have implemented the same standard.

Z39.50: Z39.50 is a complicated set of protocol standards that have been implemented in many fields from banking to publishing. In libraries, it has been used mainly to allow users to enter a search in their local OPAC, using that local OPAC's native interface, and send the search out to other OPACs, retrieve results, and display them in the local OPAC's native interface once again. Implementing and setting up Z39.50 functionality that would actually work between two systems is complicated and time-consuming, and takes a lot of trial, error, and tweaking for the two systems that want to talk to each other.

One obvious problem is the incompatibility of the underlying data and data structures. If OPAC X indexes names of editors for journals and OPAC Y does not, when a query is sent from X to Y that includes a request for journal titles edited by Joe Blow, the query will come up empty even though OPAC Y may well contain a dozen such journals. That is not the fault of the technology, but rather that the two systems have not handled their data the same way. So, users may be frustrated because the apparent promise of Z39.50 is that one can search OPAC Y exactly the same as one would search one's own local OPAC X except that it isn't entirely true. Still, Z39.50 was an important step in the right direction.

OpenURL: More recently, the standard used to link different databases is called OpenURL. It's much easier to implement than Z39.50, as it uses the usual network protocols to send and receive a URL as the method of passing information. Each piece of information sent in an OpenURL is given a tag indicating what kind of information it is. Most systems don't care what order the information is sent or received, as long as each bit is correctly tagged. OpenURL makes it possible to do a search in one database, find a citation but no full-text, then click a link to send an OpenURL through an intermediary service such as SFX from Ex Libris or 360 Link from Serials Solutions to another database with the full-text. The intermediary service maintains a profile of all the full-text currently available to the library. It checks the incoming OpenURL (coming from the "referring source") and either presents the user with options from which to select or passes them directly through to full-text in another database (the "target"). OpenURL is also used to send bibliographic information from a database to an interlibrary loan service like OCLC's ILLiad, populating the request form automatically. If the intermediary service finds no full-text available to the library, then the user can choose to get the article via ILL, all using the same underlying technology.

Federated Search (Metasearch): Federated Search is the dream of every patron and every librarian: just enter your search term(s) in one place, press the button, and search everything in one shot, returning the de-duped results in relevance order. That's the dream, but the reality isn't there yet. Federated Search uses OpenURLs to send the information directly to the other databases, many at a time, then to return the results from all those searches to the originating Federated Search product. Once again, the devil is in the details, and those little incompatibilities can cause problems. The more resources one tries to search at once, the more incompatibilities there will be. The trouble is that patron expectations are higher, thinking they can search "everything" with one try, but there are many useful resources that are not capable of handling Federated Search. They are left out, but patrons think they have searched it all. Another consideration with Federated Search is the time it takes to retrieve, de-dupe (usually very imperfectly), and display the results. The more resources that are searched at once, the longer it takes to bring back results. Sometimes it takes so long the system times out. As time goes on, more resources are becoming Federated Search-capable, so it is up to the individual library to decide whether to implement a Federated Search of some but not all their resources now or wait for more players to get on board.

These services can be viewed on a continuum: at the simplest level, the user has to enter the same search in each database, reviewing each set of results individually. Any database can handle this approach. At the next level up, OpenURL linking, the user enters the search in one database, and if no full-text results are found, the user can forward the search on to the intermediary service to see if full-text is available from some other source. Many databases are OpenURL-enabled, but there are some that get left out because they can't. At the highest level, federated searching, the user enters the Federated Search environment, enters one search that will be carried out in multiple databases, and gets back results from most of them. Some may mishandle the search or time-out; most will be de-duped (although this is far from perfect); and maybe they will be in some sort of relevance order. Most databases will not be capable of this inter-action, and some are only semi-capable, so there is a bigger gap between expectations and results. Federated Search has been implemented in many libraries, while, because of the remaining drawbacks, many others are waiting for them to mature. The decision of if and when to implement is individual to each library.

Vendor-Wide Metasearching: Several of the major vendors also offer some version of cross-searching between their products. Since they control all the content, they can insure that everything is standard, making cross-searching very easy. It can also be a marketing tool as some vendors will allow cross-searching of citations (not full-text) from their databases to which a given library does not have a subscription, in hopes of making those other databases more appealing for purchase.

As with the resources themselves, the associated technologies are also evolving, improving, and permutating into new things. Increases in interoperability and ever-increasingly seamless interactions between different developing systems will be the trend of the future with the most impact on libraries.

This is a brave new world with all kinds of creative renditions that don't fit neatly into old pigeonholes, and it will be for you to acquire them, catalog them, provide access to them, support and troubleshoot them, and manage them in every way. Be prepared to see things you have never seen before on a regular basis!

THOUGHT PROVOKERS

Consider the following questions. Discuss them with colleagues if possible.

1. Can you make a case for defining any e-resource differently than I have done above? Can you think of e-resources that might fit more than one category?
2. What's your take on the situation with article linking and federated search? Would you go straight to implementing federated search as the situation stands today? Why or why not?
3. What are the advantages and disadvantages of vendor-wide metasearching?

ASSIGNMENT ONE: DEFINING ELECTRONIC RESOURCES

Select five different electronic resources from those available or well known to you. Match each resource to one of the definitions from the chapter and explain why you think it fits. Be sure to include at least three different types of resources. Write one to two paragraphs for each resource.

2

Acquiring Electronic Resources

COLLECTION DEVELOPMENT DOCUMENTS

The first step you will take in acquiring any resource for your library is to know what you need. In fact, you may need to take a step back even further than that and know *why* you collect materials in the first place. Before you start looking for resources, you need to have a collection development document which lays out the *why* as well as the *what* and *how*.

A clear and effective collection development document will have three distinct parts: Philosophy, Policy, and Procedure. When you look at other institutions' policy documents, you may find that many don't make a distinction between these three, but instead they mix them all together in a muddled way.

Start your document with *why* you collect, that is, the underlying philosophy. This will most likely be something along the lines of "to support the curriculum" or "to support teaching, learning, and research." You should first look at the mission statement for your college or university and write your philosophy in accord with and support of that mission. In fact, your document should explicitly state that fact. If your library has a mission statement, you need to be in accord with that as well.

Once you know why you are collecting, it's time to get down to the nitty-gritty details of *what* you are going to collect. Begin with definitions of the material the policy covers. It may also be beneficial to state clearly some material the policy does *not* cover. For example, the electronic resource collection development policies at some libraries do not cover archival material in electronic format. They also may not cover physical in-house formats, such as CDs, in a pocket with a book or not. A good policy should clearly state what is covered by the policy and what is not.

The criteria for selecting specific material will be the guts of your document. You should start with the same criteria used for selecting print and physical format material, and then expand to cover the factors that make electronic resources different from print resources. Some of these considerations may include access, functionality/usability, interoperability, stability, archiving, documentation, customer support, appropriateness of format, and other possibilities. For example, your institution may wish to specify collecting only resources that can be accessed by IP address recognition and do not need a password, or you may want to indicate preferences for user-friendly interfaces, or you may want a different set of rules for single-user e-books versus multi-user e-books. Carefully consider all aspects of what makes electronic resources different, organize the features you wish to address in your policy, and lay things out in a clear and unambiguous fashion. Be prepared to update this portion of your document fairly often as future developments unfold.

Another important criterion that needs to be included in the policy portion of your document is criteria for "deselection" or withdrawal or cancellation. Lay out the circumstances that would be "red flags" indicating a given resource should be reviewed, such as a sudden large increase in cost or a disadvantageous change in interface. As with the selection criteria, organize these criteria in such a way that they can easily be used as a measuring stick to determine whether to keep or discard a given resource.

The final portion of a collection development document is the set of procedures for selecting and deselecting materials. This is the "who does what, when, and how" part of the document. Some libraries do not include this type of information in the collection development policy, but rather they include it in a departmental working manual or some similar document. Whether your institution decides to include this kind of information in your policy document or not, make sure it is very distinct from the previous two portions. The most unclear and difficult documents to use are those that mix procedure with policy and criteria as if they were all part of the same thing. They aren't; keep them separate. For the purposes of this book, the procedure portion will not be covered extensively, but rather the focus will be on the philosophy and policy portions of the document.

Assessing the needs of your institution to support the curriculum is usually not the job of an electronic resource librarian. Usually, this falls within the duties of collection development specialists, selectors, departmental liaisons, reference librarians, the director, or other content experts. An electronic resources librarian should be generally familiar with the programs and curriculum of the college or university, but he or she should defer to the subject specialists who know the needs for their area. The Electronic Resources Librarian (ERL) should work together with area specialists, who, in turn, should be working with faculty to identify products for consideration, although exactly how these relationships are structured is going to vary from institution to institution.

ACQUIRING E-RESOURCES

New products will come to your attention in a number of ways. Someone may have heard of a resource through a colleague at another school. You may receive marketing materials from your vendors through regular mail, via e-mail, from a phone call, from a visit in person, through a consortial agent, or through material picked up at a conference or meeting. Someone may have noticed a new product reviewed in a library journal. Just as with print material, content providers will be working hard to get information about their products to you for your consideration. One of your responsibilities as an electronic resources librarian is to serve as a filter for the flood of information about products, sifting through for possible gems, and filing or discarding less likely products. It actually helps to have heard of products that seem of no use today.

For example, when your college adds a new program in environmental studies next year and wants the library to provide materials to support that program, you will be glad you can remember noticing that Vendor X has a subject-specific product in that area.

CONTENT CREATORS, CONTENT PROVIDERS, VENDORS, CONSORTIAL AGENTS, LIBRARY ORGANIZATIONS AND "BUYING CLUBS"

Content begins with a creator: an author, an artist, an organization producing statistics, and so forth. When the content is going to be delivered electronically, the content creator will contract with a content provider. The terms of those contracts are very individual and can affect what the user experiences at the other end, as mentioned in the discussion of "full-text" in Chapter One.

A content provider can be a vendor, or a publisher, or any number of in-between agents. Take the content for what used to be called Psychological Abstracts, which was an important print index back in the 1980s. Various authors wrote articles for various journals that were published by the American Psychological Association (APA). The APA sold that content directly through their own interface, but they also packaged it up in a variety of ways and sold it to third-party vendors. Over the years, that content has been available through APA directly, through Ovid's SilverPlatter, through CSA, through OCLC's FirstSeach, through ProQuest, and through EBSCO. Each version of the product is slightly different depending on the contracts made along the way and how it is packaged. Each vendor may alter the content slightly in terms of the metadata they attach, how they structure the data, and what features are available through their interfaces. Also, they will all be priced differently.

In general, if you buy directly from the publisher, you don't have to pay to cover the licensing fees the third-party vendors had to pay APA to use their content. In the case of Psychological Abstracts, the APA charges the library customer distinct and separate fees for content and for licensing, so you pay the licensing fee either way. When making a decision of which version to purchase, one must also take other factors into consideration, such as that one vendor's interface may have more attractive functionality or a vendor may make the purchase of a given product part of a suite of databases they sell together for a better price through a consortial agent. Salespeople are always thinking up new ways to entice buyers, and it's for us as consumers to work through these deals to our best advantage.

Another in-between agent is called an aggregator. An aggregator may also be a vendor, but not always. The aggregator draws together any number of data streams from various content providers and packages it all together. A vendor who is also an aggregator may then deliver that aggregated content out through their interface (for example, ProQuest serves as an aggregator when they draw together content from many different publishers and journals and deliver it all through their interface in a product they call the ProQuest Research Library), or you may have an aggregator who contracts with a vendor to sell the content as a database delivered via the vendor's interface (the way BIOSIS sells the content for Biological Abstracts through any number of vendors). Each party along the way puts their own stamp on the content, which can be important to know later when you are trying to troubleshoot problems with the content.

Another important player in this path between the content creator and the end user is the consortial agent. This may be a regional library council, a regional OCLC network, or an independent group of libraries who act together to negotiate deals with content providers. For example, an academic library in Tompkins County, New York, can take advantage of offers through SCRLC (the regional library council), through Nylink (the regional OCLC network until May 2011), through NYSHEI (a New York State library advocacy organization), through Pi2 (a loosely formed coalition of institutions of higher education in New York), or through WALDO. WALDO stands for Westchester Academic Library Directors Organization, but don't let the name fool you. They accept different level members well beyond the Westchester area for the purpose of making group deals on a large selection of electronic resources. They are perfectly happy to call themselves a "buying club," unlike most consortial agents who don't like it if you refer to them that way; but the general idea is that consortia get better prices on products because they are negotiating for larger numbers of customers together. WALDO also offers centralized billing and an extra contact point for support issues. Depending on your membership agreement with WALDO, your library may be paying a small administrative fee, but the overall cost savings definitely favors the member libraries, and it is more efficient to have one big bill to pay instead of many smaller ones. Depending on where your library is located, you will have a different variety of options, but many will be similar to those in this example.

Your relationships with your vendor reps deserve careful cultivation. How each relationship works will depend on your own personal style, the personality of the sales rep, and whether or not you hit it off with the person, as well as being affected by the current status of your subscriptions and the environment at the organizations for which you each work. Some sales reps are more aggressive than others, which is sometimes their own personalities and sometimes the corporate culture. It is their job, after all, to get you to buy their products. If you know your institution's needs and budgetary situation, you will be in a better position to keep this part of the business relationship positive. Try to strike a balance; sometimes you are looking for a new product, and you are very likely to make a purchase. Your reps will always be happy to hear that! Other times you may know you can't buy anything new, which doesn't make them happy but it is what it is.

A key skill for an electronic resources librarian is saying no, diplomatically, yet firmly. This is a skill that has to be learned and adapted in your own style and can't really be taught, but it is indispensable. Make a point of being open to listening to information about new products whether you are likely to buy at that time or not, just to keep yourself informed about what is available should your situation change. Also, let the reps fill you in on updates to current products as well as future enhancements. Be professional, be polite, and be friendly if you like, but don't be pushed around or intimidated. Always remember that you have the power to say yes or no. Let that fact give you confidence to respond with courtesy and firmness.

Besides selling you products, vendors should be responsive when there is a problem. Some vendors will have different people to handle customer service or tech support, while with other vendors all of that is funneled through the sales rep. You'll have to learn the setup for each company. Over time you'll also learn which companies have good customer service and which could use improvement. You can make that a factor when selecting new products to purchase; or when making a decision about switching vendors for the same product. If you are unhappy, let them know. Do it politely, listen to explanations if any are given, but if you are truly unhappy, be firm and insist on better service. Most vendors value good customer relations and will want to work to make you satisfied so you will want to continue being their customer. Down the line, when you have a problem that needs addressing, a company will be more likely to go the extra mile for you if you have taken time to form a positive relationship beforehand. It's also just more pleasant to work with people with whom you have good relations.

COMPARISON SHOPPING AND GETTING THE BEST DEAL

Oftentimes, the database you want will be available from several vendors. Obviously, you will want to compare the price from each vendor, but there are other factors to consider as well. Just because the databases seem to be the same, sometimes they aren't. Sometimes one vendor gets a slightly different package from the content provider, so if the exact makeup of the database is important to you, ask lots of questions about specific content. Vendors don't like to admit their product is lacking anything, so you really have to be savvy about this. Some of them will have enhancements, added information, or features. Take a look at those and decide if any of them make the difference that counts for your institution. Sometimes those bells and whistles are really useful; sometimes they are just bells and whistles. Set up a trial and let your subject specialists try out different databases, both for interface functionality and to sample the content. You may want to pay slightly more to switch vendors because you hate the old product's interface, or you may choose between similarly priced offers because you already have a lot of things in one interface. This way your users don't have to learn quite as many different environments. You may see products you led to believe are "the same," but when you look closely at the content, you find they lack a piece which is critical to you.

The price a vendor gives you is not always set in stone. Occasionally they will have wiggle room to make a deal. Maybe they will offer you a better price if you buy two products or if you agree to a three-year commitment. For example, vendor reps may tell you they can't give you a price break on a particular new product, but if you bought it at the list price, they might be able to give you a cut on one of the products to which you already subscribe. Sometimes these are great deals, but always look them over carefully. Remember, for example, that if you commit to continuing your subscription for three years, you can't later cancel without being in breach of a legal contract and without damaging your institution's reputation and chances for making future deals. Sometimes those two- and three-year deals require you to pay upfront in the first year. You will usually get a really good price but it can be tough on your budgeting. You'll have to come up with a lot of money this year, and for the next couple of years it will seem like you have extra money; but then in the 4th year, you suddenly have to pay again, and the price will have gone up each year. Another feature you will sometimes see in multiyear deals is a price increase cap, where the annual increase is guaranteed not to be more than a certain amount or is even set firmly. Those deals are great for budgets. Mostly the price you are given is the price you'll have to pay, but if you don't like it, you might diplomatically sound out your rep to see if the vendor is willing to offer you a deal.

Consortial agents, library organizations, and library "buying clubs" are also a good place to get deals on electronic resources. They will negotiate with the vendor on behalf of their members. These deals are *not* negotiable any further by the librarians. Quite often they will be the best deal available, but not always, so look them over as carefully as you would a deal made directly with a vendor. Take into consideration any membership fees you may be paying. If the only benefit of a $2,000-a-year membership with Library Organization X is a deal that saves you $250, it would be better to forego the membership and buy directly. On the other hand, paying $500 for a membership through which you can take advantage of a dozen deals which save you thousands of dollars in addition to centralized billing is well worth the investment. Some groups charge no membership fee or only an administrative fee to let you take advantage of the deals they have struck with vendors.

Read the license carefully, particularly if it is lengthy. Look for key issues that concern your institution, such as interlibrary loan rights or remote access provisions. Confirm that the contract/license covers the correct details, such as the right number of simultaneous users and the agreed-upon price. You will find that some vendors provide separate documents for the license and for the contract or purchase commitment. Most require some sort of paperwork to be signed in advance, while some will send paperwork to be signed later. Be very wary of vendors who do not offer any written license. Sometimes that is just fine, but you can be burned when a deal doesn't go through as you expected and you realize too late that among the many papers which were exchanged, there was never any "license," so you do not have legal proof of exactly what was included in the services for which you had paid a lot of money, nor any timeline promised, nor any remedy or consequence outlined if one party does not deliver on their obligations. Reading licenses can be dreadfully boring, but you would be wise to just knuckle down and do it.

ORDER, RENEW, AND PAY

Ordering and paying for electronic resources is not all that different from paying for print subscriptions. In most cases, you let the vendor rep know that you have decided to purchase the product, just as you would let a publisher know the same thing. You confirm which deal you are taking and any other details of the offer that you feel need to be especially clear. You will want to settle on a start date. The vendor then lets you know the steps you need to take in terms of paperwork to be signed or information they need from your library. Generally, the vendor will send an invoice and you will pay in a timely fashion however your library is set up to pay invoices.

Delivery is where things are different. Instead of waiting for a physical item to arrive, you have to set up access. All the details of doing that will be covered in the chapter on providing access to electronic resources, but it is wise to confirm that access is working, both from on campus as well as from remote, before you pay the invoice (unless you were required to pay before the vendor would turn on your access to their product). If there are any problems, you will want to contact the vendor immediately to work things out, whether the issue is access or something about the product that is not what you expected, such as different functionality or missing content, for example. If you have not yet paid your bill, you'll have a bit of leverage getting things rectified, but usually vendors are anxious to make you happy and deliver what they promised.

Most electronic resource subscriptions require an annual renewal commitment. This is your opportunity to review and decide if you want to continue any given subscription. Usually, if you renew, you have to sign a renewal commitment, although purchases through consortial agreements may only require one signature for a whole slate of subscriptions you get through that consortial agent. Also like print subscriptions, some run on calendar year renewals, some run on a summertime renewal, and some start at random times during the year based on when you first placed your order. If you start a subscription in the middle of a vendor's fiscal cycle, sometimes they will ask you to either pay a smaller prorated fee from the beginning of your subscription until the end of their year, or they may give you the option to pay a larger prorated fee that covers the gap from the time you begin the subscription until the end of their year plus the whole next year.

Here's an example, in case that's confusing. Say it is August and you want to purchase a subscription to Database Y. It costs $12,000 per year, but the vendor's fiscal year runs January to December. You could wait until January to add it, but Professor X wants to use it this fall. So, you can pay the prorated price for September through December ($4,000) or you might prefer to pay $16,000 ($12,000 for an annual subscription plus the $4,000 to cover from now until the end of the vendor's fiscal year). If the gap time crosses *your* fiscal year-end, you'll have to think carefully if you prefer to pay it in this year's budget or next year's budget as well as when your institution will allow you to pay. Sometimes if not enough of the subscription falls in the current fiscal year the auditors won't let you pay in this fiscal year. Again, you'll want to look at these deals with an eye to how they affect your budgeting.

Ordering and paying for perpetually licensed items, such as databases or e-books (these are sometimes referred to as "permanent access" items although that is a bit of a misnomer), is a hybrid process, somewhere between purchasing hard copy items and purchasing electronic subscription items. You will almost certainly have to reconsider the ordering work flow to add e-books into the mix. Acquisitions staff members are generally all set up to order physical items, one title at a time, for a large portion of their work; but they are not usually positioned to deal with setting up, maintaining, or troubleshooting access to online resources. Electronic resources' staff members are experts at setting up access, but they have a lot of various jobs to do and don't usually have time to spend ordering titles one by one the way the acquisitions staff do. When your library starts licensing e-books individually, title by title, you will need to seriously rethink your ordering work flow. You may also need to edit and update your electronic collection development policy. One solution is to set up a process where the acquisitions staff members place the orders for e-books, whether directly with vendors or through an agent, such as YBP or Coutts, to be delivered via ebrary, NetLibrary, and other e-book platforms. When the staff members receive the confirmation that access has been activated, they pass off to the electronic resources people to set up access. When access has been confirmed, the electronic resources staff members let the acquisitions staff members know the bill can be paid, and the rest of the maintenance down the line can stay with the electronic resources staff. Or you may increase the number of staff in either acquisitions or e-resources and have the whole operation remain in one department or the other. Or if you are ordering very few titles, it might be handled as a one-off by the electronic resources staff. This situation will be resolved differently at each institution, so be prepared for something different anywhere you go. You should also be prepared to have to revise that work flow as the purchasing models change.

The world of electronic resources does that. Every time you think you have it all figured out, something changes and you have to adjust to handle the new situation.

SELECTED READINGS

Read at least two of these articles and answer the questions about them below.

Day, R., & Cernichiari, A. (2008). Evolving Concepts and Business Models for Acquiring Electronic Resources: An Agent and Publisher Perspective. *The Serials Librarian, 53*(4), 195–203.

Grogg, J. E., & Ashmore, B. (2009). The Art of the Deal: Negotiating in Times of Economic Stress. *Searcher, 17*(6), 42–49.

Strader, C. R., Roth, A. C., & Boissy, R. W. (2008). E-Journal Access: A Collaborative Checklist For Libraries, Subscription Agents, and Publishers. *The Serials Librarian, 55*(1), 98–116.

Whittaker, M. (2008). The Challenge of Acquisitions in the Digital Age. *Portal: Libraries and the Academy, 8*(4), 439–45.

THOUGHT PROVOKERS

Consider the following questions. Discuss them with colleagues if possible.

1. Using the insights in the Day and Cernichiari article, plus any other articles you may have read that discuss The Big Deal, and bringing in your own personal experiences, whom do you think benefits most from The Big Deal and under what conditions? Under what conditions would The Big Deal *not* be the best deal for an institution and why? What other options could a library find to get the titles they want for a price they can afford?

2. After reading the Whittaker article, select an acquisitions issue from her random sampling of challenges facing e-resource librarians and give your opinion. In particular, if you can draw ideas from her article to help choose criteria for selection, you are getting to the meat of things. The section on e-books, toward the end of the article, is particularly interesting: she is right about some things, wrong about others, and misses some key pieces, in my opinion. What do you think are the issues we face when selecting e-books?

3. From any of your other readings or experiences in the field, what are your thoughts on any of the following topics?
   • Single-user versus campus-wide access as a selection criteria
   • The Big Deal compared to custom packages or consortial deals
   • How an ERMS (Electronic Resources Management System) can assist in the acquisitions process
   • Open access/scholarly communication and its impact on acquisitions
   • SERU (Shared E-Resource Understanding) and the standardization of licensing e-resources
   • Electronic content embargoes (stated and de facto) in the print versus electronic decision-making process

4. What do you think can be negotiated by a library when purchasing an electronic resource besides the price? Or, when looking at the price, what bargaining chips might you have to get a better price? How has the recent economic downturn affected libraries' ability to negotiate with vendors for e-resources?

5. Consider all the players in the acquisition of e-resources. The Strader/Roth/Boissy article mentions some of them, and this chapter covers some more. What's the role of each of these in negotiating the deal? Are there additional layers of parties involved on the library end which we haven't considered here? The acquisitions staff, the collection development librarians, the administration of the library, and also parties outside the library—whichever branch of the administration to which the library reports—the accounting office and ITS may on occasion have something to say with regard to whether or not a product may be purchased. Think of some circumstances where some of these more peripheral players may have an impact on a deal.

CURRENT ARTICLE ASSIGNMENT

Locate and read an article on the topic of acquiring e-resources. The article should be no more than three years old and should not be one of those listed here. Write up a one-to-two paragraph summary of the article, being sure to include the author's thesis, the author's conclusion, and your own reactions to the article.

ASSIGNMENT TWO: WEBINAR AND FEATURE REPORT

Arrange a webinar from an e-resource vendor and report on the features of their product.

Select an electronic resource product available from a vendor of your choice. Contact the vendor representative for a webinar to discuss details of the product. Write up a two-to-three page "feature report," taking care to include information on all of the following: What kind of resource is it (Use the definitions in Chapter 1)? Who are the producers (the aggregators, if applicable), the vendors, and consortial agents through whom you can purchase this product? What interfaces are available? What special features does the interface have? What's the coverage? What access models are available? What features are available in the administrative module? Include any other features you feel are important, and feel free to make general observations.

Note: Be sure to ask the vendor to give you a tour of the administrative module.

ADDITIONAL READINGS ON THE ACQUISITION OF E-RESOURES

Articles

Flatley, R., & Prock, K. (2009). E-Resource Collection Development: A Survey of Current Practices in Academic Libraries. *Library Philosophy and Practice, 2009*, 1–5.

Fortini, T. (2007). Going Online: Academic Libraries and the Move from Print to Electronic Journals. *Library Student Journal, 2*(6), 3–11.

Hulseberg, A., & Monson, S. (2009). Strategic Planning for Electronic Resources Management: A Case Study at Gustavus Adolphus College. *Journal of Electronic Resources Librarianship, 21*(2), 163–71.

Miller, R. (2008). Acts of Vision: The Practice of Licensing. *Collection Management, 32*(1/2), 173–90.

Price, A. (2009). How to Make a Dollar Out of Fifteen Cents: Tips for Electronic Collection Development. *Collection Building, 28*, 31–34.

Vignau, B. S. S., & Quesada, R. L. P. (2006). Collection Development in a Digital Environment: An Imperative for Information Organizations in the Twenty-first Century. *Collection Building, 25*(4), 139–44.

Books

Conger, Joan E. *Collaborative Electronic Resources Management: From Acquisitions to Assessment.* Westport, CT: Libraries Unlimited, 2004. [Section on License Negotiation]

Gregory, V. L. *Selecting and Managing Electronic Resources: A How-To-Do-It Manual for Librarians.* New York: Neal-Shuman, 2006.

Kovacs, Diane K., & Kara L. Robinson. *The Kovacs Guide to Electronic Library Collection Development: Essential Core Subject Collections, Selection Criteria, and Guidelines.* New York: Neal-Schuman, 2004.

3

Providing Access to Electronic Resources

So you've made a deal, signed a contract or license agreement, and paid your invoice. You've purchased a database, an e-journal subscription, or an e-book. Let's use a database as an example. Unlike ordering physical items, you can't just sit back and wait for your new database to arrive. The final step in acquiring the database is to make it accessible to your patrons.

IP-ADDRESS RECOGNITION

You need to know what method of access is going to be used. The most common, and the most practical and convenient, is IP-address recognition. An Internet Protocol (or IP) address is a number assigned to any device on the internet. A college campus typically has a server, called a DNS server, which dynamically assigns an IP address to each machine as it logs onto the network from a range of numbers used only for that institution. You provide the vendor with the IP range for your campus, and the vendor will let anyone coming from an address in that range into their services without further authentication. If an ID and password are required, you'll have to find a way to communicate this information to authorized users in such a way that it is *not* communicated to non-authorized users. Because there really is no good way to do this, an ID/password access method is not practical for the campus setting; I strongly recommend you avoid it as much as possible. Another method of authenticating users is individual user registration. You give the vendor your e-mail domain (syr.edu, umich.edu), and they allow users with an e-mail address from that domain to register, each with his or her own self-selected ID and password. The vendor manages that information, which is preferable because you surely don't want to get into that business. You may also see some combination, such as IP-address plus user registration.

Access URL from Vendor

The first step will be done by the vendor: access to the resource has to be "turned on" at the vendor's end. Then the vendor has to send you access information. Usually, that is a URL link. Sometimes that link is generic; their system will be checking your IP and routing your users into the right account. Sometimes that link is created especially for your institution. Regardless, the first thing you should do when you receive the URL is test it to be sure you can get access. If you can't, start troubleshooting with the vendor right away before you make the link public.

PROXY SERVER AUTHENTICATION

When you have tested and know you can get into the resource, you need to take steps to make sure your authorized users can get in, too. Most campus networks are set up to allow remote access to authorized users by passing them through a proxy server. For example, say you are an authorized user for Syracuse University's library resources. You are trying to get into a database from a remote location, like your home. When you click the link on the library webpage, it directs you to the proxy to log in. That's because the link you used has the proxy server as a prefix, and if you are coming in from an IP address from outside the campus IP range, it will not let you through without first entering your ID and password. That information is usually authenticated by checking it against the campus LDAP, another system where all the IDs and passwords are managed. If you are on the list as an authorized user, you are passed through the proxy. What that means is that you are temporarily assigned an IP address from a pool of available numbers within the campus IP range. You now "look" like a person coming from on campus to the various services which have set up access for the campus IP range.

This isn't a technical manual on how to run network applications, but it will help you work better with whomever runs the proxy server if you have a general idea of how it works and where things can go wrong if you need to troubleshoot a problem. We'll get into that more in the chapter on providing support.

Proxy Configuration

Sometimes the job of maintaining the proxy server falls to an electronic resources librarian, sometimes it does not, but it always requires coordination with campus IT/Network support. The proxy is set up with entries for each service. Often you need only one entry per vendor, and it will work for all their products. Sometimes you need individual entries for specific products. The entry in the proxy configuration points to an address and a domain, so if the vendor uses one server for the entry point to their service but then uses load-balancing to shift the incoming requests for data to other servers, you could have a problem if those other servers are set up on different domains.

You can set a proxy to use a wild card, like *.ebscohost.com instead of specifying each server in that group. You should use that kind of entry as often as possible although it takes a bit more expertise in proxy management to set it up. It will be your job to get the correct proxy information from the vendor to the person who manages the proxy server (or into the proxy configuration yourself, if that is your job). Once it is in the proxy and the server has been rebooted, you will want to test access from a remote location. If there are problems, you'll be the go-between to coordinate the troubleshooting between the vendor and the campus IT. Here is a mock-up sample EZproxy configuration entry as it would be laid out for an individual resource:

T: SPORTDiscus
U: http://search.ebscohost.com
D: *.ebscohost.com

T is for Title and is for human purposes—the EZproxy doesn't need a name to make the linking work. U is for URL and D is for Domain. Sometimes you will see H for Host, which seems to work very similarly to Domain. When maintaining the proxy configuration files became my responsibility during a period when we had a vacancy in the library systems position, it seemed advantageous to put a comments field in every entry with the date the entry was added and the person who added it, and the same for any significant changes to an entry. When that work was turned over to our new person, everything in the configuration file was tidy and annotated to make it easier for him to see what was what. If you find yourself in a position where you have to manage a proxy server, you'll want to learn a lot more about it than this sketchy example.

Let's say everything has gone smoothly, and you have access on campus and from remote locations. How do you make the access available to your users?

OPAC ACCESS

You have a variety of possible ways to provide access. The most obvious one is through your online catalog. Most libraries have bibliographic records in their catalogs for databases and e-journals to which they subscribe, as well as for e-books, whether they have been perpetually licensed or are subscriptions. Some libraries upload records regularly for titles in aggregated databases as well. Usually this is done by subscribing to a MARC record service from your holdings management company, such as Serials Solutions or TDNet. It's still labor-intensive because titles come and go from aggregated databases on a near-daily basis, which means monthly (or more frequent) uploads and deletions to keep up with the changes. It does provide a lot more visibility for those titles; but it is never going to be up-to-the-minute accurate information. My college does not include these titles in our OPAC, but this is the choice of each individual library.

856 Link

MARC records have a field for URLs, the 856. The 856 has subfields for the link as well as for the link text. If your institution uses a proxy server, you must include the proxy string in front of the access URL (sometimes called a "proxy pre-pend") in order for off-campus users to be able to get to the resource. Sometimes the 856 is placed in the bibliographic record, while other libraries put it in the holdings record (MFHD). Here is a sample 856, with the proxy string in front and the link text in subfield 3:
‡u
   http:ezproxy.ithaca.edu:2048/login?url=http://search.ebscohost.com/login.aspx ?authtype=ip,uid&profile=ehost&defaultdb=s3h ‡3 Connect to SPORTDiscus

URL MAINTENANCE

An issue that comes up frequently when talking about putting URLs into catalog records is URL maintenance. As websites change and links break, who keeps the hundreds of URLs in your catalog up to date? Some Integrated Library Systems (ILS) have "link-checking" software, but it is very rudimentary, and I have found that it misses most errors. If it checks and the link goes somewhere, even if it goes to the totally wrong place, the software assumes everything is fine and doesn't report it as an error to be corrected. Better link-checking software is available for websites, but these won't run inside your ILS. Right now, the only way to do a thorough check of your links is to do it one-by-one by hand. A student can do link-checking, but even that is a very labor-intensive and long-term project. The most common approach among libraries is to just fix the ones that get reported. If no one notices that a link is broken, it's not getting enough use to be worth the trouble to fix it. Spend your limited maintenance time fixing things people are actually using.

PORTALS

Another way to provide access to electronic resources is through a library portal. A portal can be as simple as a static webpage with an A-to-Z list of links to your databases, or it can be a fully featured, searchable service that constantly tracks changes to your aggregated holdings, or it can be a system that allows the user to create custom lists of resources on the fly. A "discovery layer" is also a form of portal.

Static Webpage

The static A-to-Z list was the earliest version of a portal. It remains the cheapest way to provide access, so you will find many schools with smaller budgets still using this method. It's not practical for an institution with dozens of databases, but it works well enough for the smaller schools' smaller holdings.

HOLDINGS MANAGEMENT SERVICE

Perhaps the most popular way of providing access to databases is through a holdings management service, such as Serials Solutions or TDNet. The library indicates to which databases and e-journals it subscribes, and Serials Solutions does the rest. They keep track of all the holdings changes within aggregated databases, name changes, and so forth, and they provide the library's users with an up-to-date, searchable listing of journals to which the library has access. Users can browse the list A-to-Z, or they can type a title or part of a title in a search box to zero in on the desired title. If the library staff chooses to send print and microform serials holdings to Serials Solutions to be included in the library's profile, these can be searched simultaneously with electronic journals, returning complete results of any and all formats the library can provide. Such holdings management services may also have a feature allowing the user to search the library's electronic holdings according to subject area. This kind of service does not cover A&I databases, so a librarian may feel the need to offer access yet another way.

DYNAMIC CUSTOMIZED ACCESS:
HOME-GROWN OR OPEN SOURCE SYSTEMS

A more recent kind of portal is one librarians build themselves, customized to meet the specific user needs of the institution. Originally, only large schools or tech schools had the resources, in terms of technical experts as well as financial support, to create their own in-house systems. A few years ago, East Carolina University made the code available for their subject guide software for free: a portal they called Pirate-Source (named for the school mascot). Eventually the lead developer moved on and East Carolina stopped supporting it. My former colleague, Andrew Darby, who was Web Services Librarian at Ithaca College for several years, took the lead in developing, documenting, licensing, and distributing the software, greatly enhanced and renamed SubjectsPlus, to any library that wants to download it.

SubjectsPlus will work out of the box with minimal branding or customization, or you can get right under the hood and adjust it to do what your heart desires, while a community of fellow users acts as tech support and development partners. A local database of records underlies a number of SubjectsPlus functions, one of which provides an A-to-Z list of databases (full-text or not) or any other resource you care to include on that list, while another function allows the user to dynamically create custom subject-based lists of specific kinds of resources, including print, websites, and any other kind of resource, not just electronic ones, on-the-fly in seconds. The custom lists come with a pop-up of top recommended resources, information for contacting the local subject librarian, and other supplementary help selected by that librarian, all organized and presented neatly. A backend interface allows librarians to add and manage resources they want to see on the subject guides they create without needing technical assistance, so the whole system is very user-friendly.

You can see the implementation of SubjectsPlus at Ithaca College at: http://www.ithacalibrary.com/subjects/, or for the database list, see: http://www.ithacalibrary.com/research/databases.php. Or visit the SubjectsPlus webpage: http://www.ithacalibrary.com/subsplus/. This kind of free, collaborative community development of library services is making it possible for even small libraries with limited expertise and resources to bring a high level of service to their patrons.

COMMERCIAL PORTALS

Of course there are commercial portals a library can purchase and implement. One popular product is LibGuides from Springshare. If you are interested in pursuing it further, you might have a look at this information:

http://www.schoollibraryjournal.com/article/CA6628338.html
http://journal.lib.uoguelph.ca/index.php/perj/article/view/907/1351

Another trend on college campuses is for the college to provide some sort of MyHome page for students and faculty. So, you might have MyIthaca at Ithaca or MySlice at Syracuse. Depending on the functionality of the software running these MyHome pages, users may be able to create their own custom portals to resources they use often.

LIBRARY WEBPAGES

Your library's webpage is a portal to all manner of resources, including electronic resources, but also print and human (reference) resources as well. This meta-level portal is not usually the responsibility of the electronic resources librarian (although it may be), but that person will want to be sure e-resources are featured prominently on this page. At some libraries, widgets allow users to search the OPAC, the database list, or the journal list all from the library's top webpage.

METAPORTALS

The term *MetaPortals* is my creation for lack of a better descriptor. I use it to describe integrated commercial discovery layer products, such as Ex Libris' Primo or Serials Solutions' Summon. They try to be everything to everyone, and a portal to all, like a federated search on steroids with MyHome thrown in. Several of these products have come out recently and will be the wave of the future if vendors have their way. They tend to be very pricey, take a *lot* of work to implement, and, like any other form of federated search, many resources are not ready to operate at that level and are not compatible. The concept is terrific, but these products are still in their infancy. Time will tell whether they catch on and everyone has to have one or if people move more toward user-community-supported open source software.

SERVERS AND IT RELATIONS

A library does need a PHP (a general purpose scripting language) server on which to run SubjectsPlus, which brings us to a very important ingredient in terms of providing access to electronic resources, the library's relationship with campus IT or network services. This is a mission-critical relationship for libraries and librarians and needs to be carefully cultivated, as you'll find that conflict comes up very easily. In my experience, most librarians understand and respect the value of the skills that IT folks bring to the table, but IT workers tend to be less inclined to respect the value of a librarian's skills. This often leads to resentments on both sides. You've got to work past those barriers and do your best to build a cooperative partnership with IT, especially if you ever want to get any of those special projects off the ground. Hopefully, in time, more IT people will value our work in support of the mission of the institution. My view is surely prejudiced but based on my own personal experience, you will find many other librarians with similar views. Correct or biased, it's a situation with which you will need to deal if you work in an academic library.

Every campus is organized differently, but you'll only rarely find a library that has its own library IT staff that is entirely independent of the general campus IT. Most usually have some variation on the division of labor. At many colleges, all servers are owned, housed, and run by IT. If you want a new machine, you have to go through IT, get their approval, and get it on their budget. Needless to say, in most colleges, it is very, very difficult to get a new server or even to provide a new service on an old server. Once you have one, any ongoing maintenance costs do not have to come out of your budget. This is just one variation. Some librarians can buy their own servers and run them themselves, but they have to coordinate with IT to put services behind the campus firewall. Some share server duties or split them up in unique ways. Things can get very territorial if you are not sensitive to the position of your colleagues in IT. If you find yourself in an electronic resources librarian position, you will want to learn the hierarchy and the relation of IT to the library.

One clever work-around to the server issue is to go "off-shore" for your needs. If you wanted to add SubjectsPlus, for example, and you could not get permission to run PHP on one of the IT servers at your institution, even if you offered to pay for a new machine, you might be able to rent commercial server services. It only costs us about $10 a month, and you can run whatever services you want on your server. Our server is www.ithacalibrary.com, and users move back and forth from www.ithaca.edu/library to www.ithacalibrary.com without even knowing they are on two different servers. It has worked out very well.

E-JOURNALS

Now you know how to successfully order and provide access to a new database. What about e-journals? You will find many similarities in setting up access to individual e-journal subscriptions, but there are differences as well.

Registration

When you are adding a new e-journal subscription, you still need to provide an IP range to the vendor and get access information back from them just as you would with a database, but often, you also have to "register" the title. If your e-journal subscription is through an agent, such as EBSCO, they will have their own process for adding titles, but they'll also have support to help you. If you are purchasing directly from a publisher, you may have to register with their site in a similar fashion. Even if you have made the purchase through an agent, some publishers require you to register with them as well as the agent. You may run into anomalies that require some other piece of unexpected work. As with anything else having to do with electronic resources, each one is different.

Similar to databases, you still have to be sure your proxy access is set up and your holdings management service has the information they need to include the journals in the searchable journal title list. The Serials Solutions product is called the E-Journal Portal, Ex Libris' product is called SFX, but regardless of the product they have, most libraries give it their own custom name.

E-BOOKS

E-books are a curious breed. In some ways, they are like regular print books, but in other ways, they are more like databases. They present some interesting challenges for acquisitions and access.

Subscription Packages and Reader Software

E-books can be purchased as part of a subscription package in which case setting up access is almost entirely like setting up access for a database, although it may also require the installation of separate reader software. If it does, you will have to decide if you want to leave it entirely up to the end users, or if you want to have the latest version installed on the public access computers. This is another area where you may find yourself working closely with IT.

At many institutions, security on public machines is achieved through "imaging." That means that every time a machine is restarted, the whole thing is wiped clean, and a fresh version of everything on it is reloaded. So, if someone downloads and configures software on a given machine today, it will be wiped out and gone tomorrow, and fresh renditions of the software on the "image" for that machine will be reinstalled. This prevents users from crashing machines with malicious downloads. Security of public machines is not generally the concern of the electronic resources librarian, but this "imagining" approach has an impact on our work. If your institution uses "imaging" for security on public machines, you will need to work with IT to make sure they have the latest versions of various helper software to include on the "image" so those versions are always there for your users in the library.

Academic Complete is a large e-book package from ebrary. Until recently, the use of ebrary required the downloading and installation of their special reader software. Now they have two downloadable readers *and* a web browser version. It doesn't quite have the full functionality of the reader client yet, but it also does not require any installation. The client reader's functionality is worth the extra effort to set it up.

Another e-book package is Oxford Reference Online Premium that affords savings in terms of print reference works that could only be used on the premises, one user at a time. Because reference titles are so expensive when purchased individually, the number of titles a library can offer is limited. This package offers all those titles and more to unlimited simultaneous users anywhere, anytime. Oxford content is also accessible through a web browser with no special hardware or setup.

E-Books Purchased Individually

E-books can also be purchased individually, title by title, with a lot of options in terms of interface and setup. In fact, it seems like every few days, some e-book vendor is offering a new twist. Perpetual licenses to individual e-book titles can be purchased through ebrary, NetLibrary, Books 24/7, and other vendors, as well as directly from individual publishers. Let's take ebrary as an example. So long as you have a subscription to any of their collections, you do not pay anything more to access individually licensed titles through the ebrary platform, and there isn't much to setting up access. You must confirm that access via ebrary is working and then add a bibliographic record with the access URL in the 856 field to the OPAC. Should you ever cease to subscribe to any ebrary collection, you would have to decide if you wanted to take the raw content as a file and find a way to deliver it yourselves or if you want to pay a smaller annual access fee to continue using the ebrary platform for your individual perpetual license titles. The purchasing deal may vary slightly from vendor to vendor, but the basic setup is going to be roughly the same.

Oxford Reference publishes both print and electronic reference works that can be purchased both individually and in packages. In a recent promotion, titles were offered with the option of access through an existing subscription to Oxford Reference Online, through ebrary, or even through ScienceDirect for some titles. It may be possible to purchase one title and have it available through multiple platforms.

More recently, Congressional Quarterly is starting to offer some of their titles delivered on the library's choice of a number of different platforms, not just their own. This is a trend that would be good to see continued and expanded: the library can choose to have any title from any publisher delivered on any platform according to the library's choice. Ask your content providers if they have reciprocal agreements with other companies to allow the user the choice of both content and platform; keep telling them it's what you want.

In New York State, the State Library offers the NOVEL program that provides access for any library in the state to a number of useful databases and other electronic resources. One of these was the Gale Virtual Reference Library (GVRL). New York State libraries could purchase individual reference titles from Gale to be delivered via GVRL. Due to New York State budget cuts, NOVEL ceased to include GVRL, which meant libraries that had added on individual Gale titles had to worry if they'd lose access to them. Fortunately, that wasn't the case this time, but in tough economic times, these types of cuts can be like ripples in a pond, and librarians will sometimes have to scramble to find a way to keep access to resources they thought were all settled.

Individual titles can be like little orphans until you "place" them in a "home" on some platform. Sometimes there is only one platform available; other times a publisher will offer access through a choice of platforms. It is likely that there will be many more permutations in the future, both in terms of combinations of publishers and platform vendors and in terms of pricing and access models.

ELECTRONIC RESOURCES MANAGEMENT SYSTEMS (ERMs)

One more place where you may have to update to include access is in your Electronic Resources Management system (ERM), if you have one. Some ERMs have a public interface or an interface for public services staff, which is yet another access point. Some do not; those still have to be updated, but not for access purposes. Each one of these systems is very different even though they all use the same standards from the DLF ERMI (Digital Library Federation E-Resource Management Initiative) group, so you will have to check with the vendor of the ERM on how to do updates and then figure out your own work flow. There are also homegrown ERMs out there, most notably a fairly new one being shared for free, created by two librarians from the University of Wisconsin La Crosse, William Doering and Galadriel Chilton.

DISPLAY DESIGN AND USABILITY TESTING

One further access issue has to do with the effectiveness of the design of the access points. If you are presenting an access point in your OPAC, how does it display in the bibliographic record? Does the user understand how to get to the resource? This is where usability testing is indispensable. For example, instead of having a group of librarians sitting around a room hypothesizing and opining that users would love to have a table of contents link so they can decide ahead if they want to use a given resource, you might do usability testing with real students first. If you wait until after your systems person changes the display to move the Table of Contents (TOC) link closer to the top of the bibliographic record display in the OPAC, you might discover that students are confused by the two links and often click on the first one thinking it will take them to the resource, then get frustrated when it doesn't or annoyed that they have to take an extra step to get where they want to go. That's a hypothetical example, but it makes the point. Changes in display designed to improve access should be done with solid evidence that the change will be for the better! You might be surprised how often changes like this are made on some librarian's whim or anecdote. Usability testing is a powerful tool to aid in decision making, particularly for the electronic resources librarian in terms of how we present access points to the resources.

WHAT'S IN A NAME?

At the risk of going off on a tangent, one more issue is related to how to present electronic resources to the user. A few years back, there was intense debate over what to call electronic resources when interacting with students and other users. Everyone agreed that "electronic resources" was rather vague and mostly meaningless to our users. We would frequently get inquiries about electronic reserves from confused faculty. Some places changed their links to questions: "Looking for an article?" even for databases of images and statistical information. Others decided to call them all "Databases" even though some resources were "journal collections" or some other kind of electronic resource. Many different approaches were tried, but most interesting is that when usability testing of the names was done, they *all* confused the patrons. Students don't generally use "resources" to describe anything. They use the word "databases" as a much more broad term than we do, and they don't understand the distinction between finding articles in databases and looking up specific journal titles, even though these are very different functions on library webpages. In fact, some students use the term "journal" interchangeably with the term "article." John Kupersmith, a reference librarian at the University of California at Berkeley, manages a webpage (http://www.jkup.net/terms-studies.html) with a table of which terms worked and which didn't at various institutions. When he first posted the table on the page, nearly all of the terms appeared in both columns. That is to say, a term that worked at one school didn't work at another and vice versa. However, the table has been updated and now "database" would seem to be universally not working as a term to describe what we manage. The only way to resolve the issue is to test your own user population and use your own local data to make the decision for your school. It doesn't seem to be the case that an electronic resource by any other name smells as sweet!

SELECTED READINGS

Read at least two of these articles and answer the questions about them below.

Cole, L. (2009). The E-Deal: Keeping Up to Date and Allowing Access to the End User. *The Serials Librarian, 57*(4), 399.

Fuller, K., Livingston, J., Brown, S. W., Cowan, S., Wood, T., & Porter, L. (2009). Making Unmediated Access to E-resources a Reality: Creating a Usable ERM Interface. *Reference & User Services Quarterly, 48*(3), 287–301.

Lawrence, P. (2009). Access When and Where They Want It: Using EZproxy to Serve Our Remote Users. *Computers in Libraries, 29*(1), 6–7, 41–43.

Resnick, T., Ugaz, A., Buford, N., & Carrigan, E. (2008). E-resources: Transforming Access Services for the Digital Age. *Library Hi Tech 26*(1) 141–56.

Tonkery, Dan. (2009). Publishers, Agents, Users, and Libraries: Coming of Age in the E-World, *The Serials Librarian, 57*(3), 253–60.

THOUGHT PROVOKERS

Consider the following questions. Discuss them with colleagues if possible.

1. What role does the user community play in improving access to electronic resources using either EZproxy or SubjectsPlus? How do products like these impact the usual commercial products on the market?

2. How does the "Big Deal" potentially affect the end user's ability to access articles? What can libraries do while setting up access to keep the problems to a minimum? In many ways this question is very similar to the one I asked in a previous chapter, but let's add this twist—What parties are involved in the process who can either aid or impede the user's success in accessing articles?

3. What are some of the stumbling blocks that impede user access? Aside from troubleshooting problems after they happen (which will be covered later), are there ways we can do a better job setting up access to avoid running up against the stumbling blocks *before* they happen?

4. What do you think are the advantages and disadvantages of subscribing to e-journals directly from the publisher as compared to subscribing through an agent, particularly in terms of access?

5. What are some features of good portal design? What features do you think could use improvement over what you usually see, or are there any which should be abandoned?

CURRENT ARTICLE ASSIGNMENT

Locate and read an article on the topic of providing access to e-resources. The article should be no more than three years old and should not be one of those listed here. Write up a one- or two-paragraph summary of the article, being sure to include the author's thesis, the author's conclusion, and your own reactions to the article.

ASSIGNMENT THREE: PORTALS AND ITS

Report on an access portal, its place in the campus technology infrastructure, and the library's relationship with IT.

How does the institution with which you are most familiar deliver access to electronic resources to its library patrons? Aside from the catalog, is there an access portal? That portal could be anything from a static webpage with an alphabetical list to a sophisticated system with many features for searching a wide variety of resources creating guides on the fly, and more. Interview the person who manages the portal. Ask about the features, underlying technology, and how it works? How does the portal fit in with other online services available from the institution. Be sure to ask questions about the library's relationship with the institution's Information Technology department. Write up a three- to five-page report on what you learn, as well as your own observations on the portal *and* the arrangements with IT.

ADDITIONAL READINGS ON PROVIDING ACCESS TO E-RESOURCES

Brown, C. C., & Meagher, E. S. (2008). Cataloging Free E-Resources: Is It Worth the Investment? *Interlending & Document Supply, 36*(3), 135–41.

Byerley, S. L., Chambers, M. B., & Thohira, M. (2007). Accessibility of Web-based Library Databases: The Vendors' Perspectives in 2007. *Library Hi Tech, 25*(4), 509–27.

Chilton, G., & Doering, W. (2009). ERMes: Open Source Simplicity for Your E-Resource Management. *Computers in Libraries, 29*(8) 20–25.

Dinkelman, A., & Stacy-Bates, K. (2007). Accessing E-books Through Academic Library Web Sites. *College & Research Libraries, 68*(1), 45–58.

Eggleston, H., & Ginanni, K. (2009). Simplifying Licensed Resource Access Through Shibboleth. *The Serials Librarian, 56*(1), 209–14.

Fuller, K., Livingston, J., Brown, S. W., Cowan, S., Wood, T., & Porter, L. (2009). Making Unmediated Access to E-Resources a Reality: Creating a Usable ERM Interface. *Reference and User Services Quarterly, 48*(3), 287–301.

Harcourt, M. W., & Wolley, I. (2007). Automated Access Level Cataloging for Internet Resources at Columbia University Libraries. *Library Resources & Technical Services 51*(3), 212–25.

Lawrence, P. (2009). Access When and Where They Want It: Using EZproxy to Serve Our Remote Users. *Computers in Libraries, 29*(6), 41–43.

Llona, E., Craft, E., Yakota-Carter, K., & Pham, D. (2004). Providing Access to Foreign Language Electronic Resources. *Foreign Language Electronic Resources, 23*(3), 119.

O'Hara, L. H. (2007). Providing Access to Electronic Journals in Academic Libraries. *The Serials Librarian, 51*(3), 119–28.

Tank, E., & Frederiksen, C. (2007). The Daisy Standard: Entering the Global Virtual Library. *Library Trends, 55*(4), 932–49.

Tenopir, C. (2010). E-Access Changes Everything. *Library Journal, 135*(1), 26.

4

Administering Electronic Resources

LICENSES

Even with experience with electronic resource licenses, this author is not a legal expert. This chapter is written in layman's terms, but if, after reading it, you have doubts or concerns, you should check with your institution's legal counsel for advice.

To give you information from sources with more expertise in e-resource licenses, three other documents will be referenced here. One is a license template. Next is a webpage with more detailed information about SERU, an interesting new development in standardized licensing. The third is a document on principles for electronic resource licenses from the Association of Research Libraries and should be read as part of this chapter.

Licenses for electronic resources come in a wide variety, from the extremely simple common license, such as the half sheet with a couple of paragraphs, downloaded from a website, which was good for any database purchased by any institution from that vendor, to the dense, lengthy, and complicated, such as the quarter-inch thick stack from Elsevier for ScienceDirect, which requires two fully executed originals. Some, despite their length, are clear and straightforward, while others are entirely vague. Annual Reviews offers a license written in straightforward non-legalese language with rights, obligations, limits, warranties, and general terms, along with an invoice of the exact titles briefly but clearly covered and a place for the parties to sign and date the agreement. On the other hand, institutions purchasing subscriptions to EBSCO products through the consortial agent, WALDO, don't actually *have* a license with EBSCO for those products. EBSCO makes a license agreement with WALDO as a consortial agent, with no information as to how that agreement trickles down to individual WALDO members who purchase subscriptions to particular databases.

The basic function of a license is to protect both parties in a deal. To varying degrees, electronic resource licenses lay out who the parties are, what product was purchased, how it may be used, how it may *not* be used, who can use it, and any and all other terms and conditions of the sale or subscription. Finally, licenses often also lay out the penalties for breaking the contract, the "remedies."

Let's take a look at a template for an electronic resource license. You will find one in Appendix B or type the link below into your browser. This document is from licensingmodels.com (a joint venture of EBSCO, Harrassowitz, and Swets) and is written for electronic journals, but it has most of the basic components that apply to databases as well.

http://www.licensingmodels.org/SingleAcademicInstitutionLicense.html.

As with most legal documents, it starts with *what* the document is (an agreement between parties), the *date* of the agreement, and the parties involved. When you get to the "whereas," this is what both parties agree under the terms and conditions that follow. Then you'll usually have some definitions. For example, just who *is* an authorized user under the terms of this contract? How does this agreement define "library premises"?

After the *definitions*, we get to the meat of the document—what is it to which the two parties are agreeing, exactly? You will usually find the length of time the contract will be in effect, when it will begin, the fee, and sometimes also some information on what the licensee can keep when the contract ends.

This will usually be followed by *usage rights*, as well as *usage restrictions* and prohibitions. Some licenses have "*performance obligations*" (or "undertakings") of both parties. You may have sections on *fees/payments* and *terms/renewals*. Contracts may have "*warranties*" (we usually call them "guarantees" when we are speaking informally, but this is a very formal legal document), with indemnities and liabilities all spelled out.

Licenses usually have a *general* section where they lay out all the other terms and conditions not covered elsewhere. Finally, at the bottom, there will be a place to print the name of the authorized persons representing each party and spaces for their titles, their *signatures*, and the date each signed the document.

Some licenses will include attached documents with information: a schedule of prices, lists of titles included (not for aggregated databases, because they change all the time) and possibly even technical information, like the IP range to which the vendor will provide the service. (Most of that information is exchanged via e-mail or some other form, but some licenses include it.) For what should you be looking as you slog your way through this dense, boring document all written in legal language? Do read it all, even though it is dull and dry as dust. Keep an eye out for anything that sends up a red flag for you. Is it important to your institution that you be able to send articles from this journal or database out on interlibrary loan? Check to see if it is allowed and if there are any conditions or restrictions. Do you have to prevent walk-in users from accessing the database? Not many licenses prohibit walk-ins any more, but there have been restrictions to walk-ins in the past. Another area often of interest is what happens if and when you decide to cancel a subscription. Do you retain rights to anything? If you do, in what form? Do you get continued access to a limited portion, or do they just send you a file and you can figure out how you'll deliver it to your users?

The Association of Research Libraries (ARL) has a very useful document which includes 15 principles for licensing electronic resources. These can serve as a checklist when reviewing a license, so you may want to save this document for future use. The original document was written in 1997, but it has been updated as recently as June 2009.

You can find the document in Appendix C or access it at: http://www.arl.org/sc/market-place/license/licprinciples.shtml.

The ARL document stresses how a license is likely to restrict your use of a product. While this is true, a license also protects your library. Be suspicious of any vendor who won't give you a license. You may think that it's a good idea not to have anything in writing which would restrict your use of a resource, *but* you also don't have any protections in place for your benefit either.

As an example, we bought a hot, new electronic records management (ERM) system a few years ago. It was pricey, and we spent a lot of time going over what features we wanted to include in the deal. Negotiations with the sales representative continued for weeks to get the price down to something agreeable. Finally, the price was settled as well as which features were needed and which were not needed, and a price quote was offered. The quote was accepted and the work of implementation was started. For our library, this was complicated by the size of our server. It was too small to have both our ILS and the new ERM on the same machine. A new server was needed, bringing with it all the trouble of coming up with the additional money, permission from IT, migrating the ILS to the new machine, and other challenges.

The server and our installation were completed, although they were repeatedly delayed. The next step was getting the ERM loaded and working. There were more delays. There were unpleasant surprises about what the system included, and what it didn't, and there were also additional expenses because the salesperson didn't have her details straight. Going back through the correspondence and paperwork, we found there had never been a contract or a license, just a written price quote. In the most vague, general terms, that piece of paper indicated that we paid a certain price for a product. It gave the name of the product and not much else. A certain amount was paid for a service agreement, a contract which detailed what they would cover. That was all. It did not spell out what our ERM would include, what additional services we would have to purchase to get it loaded and running, how we could or could not use it, no guarantee that they'd stick to a particular timeline or what legal rights we had if they didn't. All of that was left vague. A license or contract was needed.

After months of being shuffled around and dodged, it became clear that they would not give us anything in writing that clearly stated what we'd bought nor would they make any guarantees or promises or lay out any penalties for not delivering what we *thought* we'd purchased. It was too late. The deal was done without a contract.

We made our deal in April 2005. It was still not fully implemented when the vendor ceased to support it in December 2008, and we were not the only customer unable to fully implement the product. We were not alone. We eventually had to uninstall it because it conflicted with the next upgrade to our ILS and even that took months to schedule with the vendor. In the end, the vendor was bought out by another company, and that was the end of it. All that time and money went for nothing but grief.

Let the buyer beware. That license is as much for your protection as the vendor's. Make sure you get what you want in writing before the deal is sealed.

More recently, a group of libraries and publishers began working on an initiative they call Shared E-Resource Understanding (SERU). The idea is that license negotiation takes too much time and costs too much overhead that could be reduced if librarians and publishers would agree to a common, standard set of terms and conditions that could be applied across many different resources from many different publishers for any and all of their customers. By agreeing in advance to the basics, the whole license negotiation thing could be bypassed, saving grief and time for all parties involved. Here is the "Problem Statement" from the SERU page on the National Information Standards Organization (NISO) site:

The current process of customer-by-customer, bilaterally negotiated formal legal contracts increases the cost of sales for both libraries and publishers and delays access for users at subscribing institutions. In some circumstances bilateral negotiation of a formal license agreement is in the interest of the publisher, the library, or both, but as the number of electronic information products expands and a lower end of the market is increasingly developed, many question whether universal, bilateral license negotiations are scalable.

Discussions with both publishers and librarians revealed a shared desire to create a new approach that involves lower overhead. Various approaches to streamlining negotiations have been tried, including the distribution of model licenses and the development by some libraries of their own standard license. While these licenses have provided a useful starting point for negotiations and have helped clarify the interests of the library community, there remains a strong sense that significant problems with the bilateral license negotiation persist.

On the side of content providers, some publishers have ceased to negotiate licenses—seemingly having simply given up on licensing and selling their e-resource products with no licenses, relying instead on existing law and their faith in community norms. Many share a perception that a negotiated license is expected by the library community for all electronic products.

At the same time, libraries struggle to manage large portfolios of licenses, to negotiate consistent terms, and to educate new publishers launching e-resources. Access to purchased resources can be significantly delayed by protracted license negotiations.

SERU Problem Statement is reproduced by permission from the National Information Standards Organization (NISO). More information about SERU is available via the NISO website at: http://www.niso.org/workrooms/seru.

SERU is an interesting development, and it is encouraging to see librarians, vendors, and publishers all sitting down together to come up with a new approach that would benefit all. Rather than each side fiercely defending its own little corner, this sort of collaboration is what has to happen for progress to occur in this arena.

If SERU is to your liking, at least for some products, and is available, then by all means, save yourself the grief. If you find something in a proposed license with which you feel your institution really can't live, then you'll want to negotiate; but you may find yourself in the position that the licenses presented by your vendors are perfectly acceptable as is, and all you have to do is read them to be sure, and sign your name. No extra time or cost in overhead is needed. Whichever approach you decide to take when the time comes for you to sign a license, take time to consider carefully, and consult your institution's legal counsel if you come up against something sticky.

Another area of cooperative work with electronic resource licenses is in the standardization of the language used to make it easier to get the data into an ERM system. As it stands, a person has to carefully read the license, interpret the meaning, and manually enter the details into an ERM. The Digital Library Federation Electronic Resource Management Initiative (DLF ERMI) group has improved that situation by at least standardizing the kind of data entry these systems are set up to receive. The next step is to talk vendors into standardizing the language they use in the licenses.

Reading through our licenses strictly to see what each one said about allowing walk-ins to use the resource, we found that almost all of the licenses that mentioned the issue allowed such access, at least under certain circumstances. However, every single one expressed it differently. In some cases, we had to sit down and read it together a couple of times to be sure we understood correctly. The main motivation for many libraries to implement an ERM is to make the terms of the license more visible and usable to reference librarians, interlibrary loan staff, and others outside the "back room," yet that aspect of ERMs is the very hardest to implement. We will look at the ERM in more detail later in this chapter.

INFORMATION TO BE MANAGED

How do we keep track of all the information we have about our electronic resources? How do we manage it all?

Cataloging Module

The cataloging module of an ILS can be seen as the administrative module for the OPAC. Bibliographic information about your resources is imported into your underlying database, then edited in cataloging, stored, and delivered to the public interface. The cataloging module is where you apply decisions about call numbers, locations, 856s—all the usual cataloging decisions having to do with the general structure of your records. You will want to start with your library's existing rules for cataloging nonelectronic materials, considering the differences of electronic resources and making adjustments to the policies as necessary.

OCLC

The vast majority of librarians get MARC records for their catalogs from OCLC, although there are starting to be other providers, such as SkyRiver. Every cataloger will know the methods for importing MARC records from OCLC, but this is another area where you face decisions about the different nature of electronic resources. It is a given, and part of the contract with OCLC, that, in participating member libraries, catalogers will "add their holdings" to OCLC. That means you will attach your library's OCLC symbol to the master record in OCLC so that everyone else in the world will know that your library has this item. This is crucial for interlibrary loan, but that holding information is also occasionally put to other purposes.

Many librarians choose not to include their electronic resource holdings for a variety of reasons. It may be because they won't lend those materials even when they are allowed to by license, or perhaps they choose to include some but not others. Many librarians do not attach holdings for items in aggregated databases because they change all the time. More recently, OCLC has been offering an E-Holdings Service, where your e-holdings management vendor will send your holdings to OCLC, who will attach and manage your aggregated and individual e-holdings for the world to see. If you have an ERM to track the licensing details for interlibrary loans and your library wants to be able to lend more electronic materials to other libraries, this might work for you. However, this is also another layer of accuracy to maintain and troubleshoot, and the main benefit is to other libraries, not to yours. This is a decision that should be made in the context of what works for your library.

MARC Records

Electronic resources are an area where significant numbers of MARC records may come from someplace besides OCLC. Some vendors have their own MARC records available, sometimes for free with the product or sometimes for an extra fee. A curious note is that they will have MARC records for the titles *within* their product but not for the product itself. MARC records are provided for all the journal titles in a given database, but not one for the database itself. For that you have to go to OCLC. This is one way that librarians can keep up with changes to the holdings in aggregated databases. They can subscribe to a MARC record service either from vendors or from their holdings management service, such as Serials Solutions.

Bulk Loading

MARC records from vendors are generally bulk-loaded and not touched individually by a human hand. That means careful attention must be paid to the bulk-loading rules. You will want to run small test batches first until you are sure the records are coming into your catalog the way you want them. You will need to work with your ILS systems person to set up any preload manipulation of the records. For example, we do a monthly bulk load of new titles from ebrary. On excellent advice from a colleague at another school who learned the hard way, we delete the titles that have been removed *before* we do the new bulk load. There are rarely more than a couple dozen deletions at most and often a lot fewer than that, so these are done by hand. Then we have a locally developed program that edits the records as they come in. MARC records are bibliographic records only, no holdings or items. The vendor, in this case ebrary, can customize our records to an extent, but they can't give us holdings records that are called MARC for Holdings Data (MFHDs, pronounced "muffheads"). Our program creates an attached MFHD for each bibliographic record, populates it with information that includes a field indicating it is an ebrary title. This makes it easier to run reports or do other bulk processing to the whole group of records in the catalog. The program grabs the 856 field, with the correct URL, out of the ebrary bibliographic and puts it into our MFHD. We get all the MARC records from ebrary free with our subscription, but one has to be prepared to do some "massaging" of the data as it is bulk loaded into a local system.

Exporting/Hooking

When you need the bibliographic information elsewhere (such as in an ERM), you will have to get it from your ILS. For some ERMs, this will mean exporting it out of the catalog and into the ERM, whether the ERM is operating locally at your institution or is hosted with the vendor. In other cases, such as if you bought your ERM from your ILS vendor, you may need to set up "hooks" between the two systems so that the ERM can "hook" into individual bibliographic records and display the information in the ERM interface. "Hooking" the systems can also allow you to see other information attached to the bibliographic record, such as acquisitions data, from the ERM interface as well.

Our ERM had some of each. We had to send vendor information, for example, to the ERM vendor to be loaded into our ERM, but we were able to set up hooks for bibliographic information. In that particular ERM, it took one more step to bring in the acquisitions information. We had to open the resource record, make sure it was hooked correctly to the right bibliographic record in the catalog, and then manually choose to link the associated acquisitions information (payment history, invoices, and so forth). Once all the pieces were set up, it was indeed very nice to have it all in one place, but it was painstaking work.

Linking Bibliographics

Another manipulation of MARC records for electronic resources that you may decide to implement is called "linking bibliographics." In some OPACs, there is functionality to link records for the same title in different formats. So, if you have a journal, let's call it the Journal of XYZ, in print, microform, and an electronic subscription as well, you can create links that will display in the OPAC so the user can see from one record display that you also have the same title in the other formats, and, what's more, the user can link over to that other record. So, if users search in the catalog and find the record for the electronic version of the Journal of XYZ, by looking at the record, they see that you only have the current five years. If they want an older article, they see the link to the print, follow it, and see that you have the issue they want in print. Be careful to watch for e-journals that have the same International Standard Serial Number (ISSN) for print and electronic versions. In some OPACs, if you use the same ISSN in both records, the link becomes circular and does not work right. Should you run up against this issue, you may be able to work around it by fudging the ISSNs. Try adding a space and an "E" to the end of the ISSN in the electronic serial record and a space and an "M" at the end of the microform record. This is a way to make the linking work without completely messing up the integrity of the ISSNs.

856s Revisited

Previously it was noted that some librarians choose to put the 856 link in the bibliographic record, while other librarians choose to put it in the MFHD. Some newer OPACs will not display the 856s that are in the MFHD. This is setting a lot of librarians scrambling. Some smaller libraries that formerly had the 856s in the MFHD are choosing to manually add a duplicate 856 to their bibliographic records, while other librarians are insisting that the vendor fix the problem. This example shows that even careful decisions made to best meet your own users' needs may have to be revisited when some external factor changes.

Acquisitions Module

The acquisitions module of your ILS is where all the financial action is tracked. Payment information, including purchase orders, invoices, payment history, and notes are entered and stored here, as well as some vendor information. You can use the serials check-in portion of the acquisitions module for your database subscriptions. That way you can keep using the same order record for a given database; you just renew the subscription each year, just as you would an annual serial publication. A database would have one order, but a new invoice for each year. There is a place to note that access has been confirmed, much as one would confirm receipt of a physical volume of a serial. You can also open one record and see the payment history back to when you first subscribed along with any notes. These records have links to records for the vendors from whom you have purchased the databases (or e-journals, or e-books, although any item with a one-time purchase is entered in acquisitions like a monograph, not like a serial). You can store vendor contact information in the vendor record: address, phone, e-mail, website, and some other details. This information can be exported, then imported into an ERM as well, although you may find it is only a tiny portion of the information you need to have on hand about each vendor. You can make the payment information visible in your ERM, but you will need to import the vendor information. Each pairing of ERMs and ILS will be a little different.

SYSTEMS MODULE

An electronic resources librarian will have to work closely with the ILS systems person. Together you will adjust settings in the systems module to support the delivery of electronic resources, set up bulk loading or any other bulk processing of records of electronic resources, help troubleshoot problems, make decisions about the display and use of e-resource MARC records from the OPAC, and to draw reports.

Reports

Many times an electronic resources librarian needs a report, particularly for projects or for annual statistics your institution has to file, or to answer questions from the library administration. For example, you may be required to give a count of the total number of e-books added in the previous fiscal year. Or you may decide you have to change the location of the 856, and you need a report of all records that contain one so you can determine if there are few enough to edit them manually or if there is some way to write a program to bulk process the change. Sometimes the decision on how to enter data in records will be driven in part by how you hope to pull information back out of the system, using reports later on down the line. Some reports can be run by the end user as a query, while others can only be run by the systems administrator. Reports are a very important tool for managing any resource, electronic or not, in the ILS.

Spreadsheets

As an electronic resources librarian, chances are you will be responsible for tracking your portion of the library budget. You'll want to watch how much has been spent in each fund, as well as how much money is left. If you find yourself with a shortage in one area, you may be able to move money from another area to cover a shortfall, although it may require working with others for approval and to actually move the money depending on how these duties are assigned at your institution. You may want your ILS systems administrator to run a report to get that kind of information into an Excel spreadsheet so you can work with it, whether you want to work with amounts transferred or amounts spent and remaining in each fund.

You will almost surely find that you won't be able to get everything you want out of your ILS in the form in which you need it. Keeping a few spreadsheets you create from scratch can be an excellent supplement to ILS reports. One I have found to be extremely useful is a spreadsheet where I have entered estimates of how much each database will cost. When I have solid information from the vendor or consortial agent, whether an actual price or a promised price increase, I enter that. If I don't, I look back over the previous years' increases and make a guess. I use this information to project the next year's costs, and then I use the spreadsheet to track the actual costs as they come in compared to the estimated costs. This method has worked quite accurately for databases. The cost of serials, whether print or electronic, is a lot more difficult to estimate because they are so hard to predict. I don't have a magic formula for that. Chat with the serials staff, consult with your e-journal subscription service providers, look over previous years' trends, then take your best guess, but be prepared to be off the mark with serials. It's just the way they are. In general, when dealing with budgetary matters, the better the information you can get and share with the person who manages the overall budget, the better you will be able to manage the resources for which you are responsible.

Spreadsheets for usage statistics may also be useful, particularly if you do not have any product that is Standardized Usage Statistics Harvesting Initiative (SUSHI)-enabled to go out and automatically harvest this data. A staff member or a student assistant can log onto each vendor's site and copy data you want into a simple spreadsheet. We'll discuss what to do with this spreadsheet in more detail in the chapter on evaluation, but for now, it is enough to know that this is yet another accumulation of important information on electronic resources that might or might not go into an ERM. You will find that you often need to create a spreadsheet—either from a report generated out of your ILS or by hand—to work out management issues, particularly but not solely for the financial aspects of administering the resources.

Electronic resources librarians have to determine their own needs and set up spreadsheets, or sometimes even homegrown Access databases, to do those tasks for which there is no existing functionality in any system or elsewhere. When loading data into an ERM, you will need to consider which of these are appropriate for inclusion and how you are going to get the data moved.

HOLDINGS MANAGEMENT SERVICE (ERAMS)

Serials Solutions is one holdings management service. These services are sometimes called ERAMS or e-resource access and management services. TDNet is another such service. Parts of Ex Libris' SFX product can be used to do some of these tasks as well. Serials Solutions 360 Core is presented here, but there may be variations depending on the service you use. The main thing a holdings management service has is a knowledge base of all current holdings in all full-text databases. What it does for libraries is to keep track of the current holdings in each of your full-text databases, including the ever-changing content of aggregated databases. Serials Solutions also allows you to upload your print and microform holdings, and you can enter your individual e-journal subscriptions as well, so your users can search your serials holdings across all formats in one place. The functionality of the portal to this information was covered in the previous chapter; this time we'll look at how it is managed.

Tracking

An ERAMS is quite complex, but it does the heavy lifting so librarians don't have to. Tracking that content, which issues of which volumes of what journals are currently available to a library's users, is the most valuable service, as there is just no way a library could do that all on its own. In some ERAMS you can customize the holdings ranges. This is not always a good plan. Once you have customized a field, it is often protected. That means that when a record is updated, those fields will not be touched. So, customize only those holdings you know you want to have to manually update from then on.

Overlap Analysis

A useful feature available in Serials Solutions 360 Core is the Overlap Analysis tool. Not only can you run analyses with in-depth details of overlapping coverage of databases to which you subscribe, but you can also run analyses of databases to which you do *not* currently subscribe, to help make purchasing decisions. One use for this tool is to compare the content of some of the big general databases, such as Gale OneFile, ProQuest Research Library, and EBSCO Academic Search Premier, to see if any of them have so much overlap and so little unique content that you would feel comfortable dropping one of them. If they manage to secure exclusive distribution rights to enough unique content, you may still want to subscribe to them all, provided the budget is available.

Client Center

The administrative interface for Serials Solutions is called the Client Center. This is where a librarian can select or deselect resources to be tracked, research information about current subscriptions or potential new products, and also make adjustments to the customizations of how the public portal functions and displays. Some features are customizable, some are not. Some you can change yourself, others you must put in a request for Serials Solutions to do it for you. You can also add new users or change permissions for users, so you can allow an assistant or colleague to access the Client Center, change permissions to allow your web services person to get in and set up interfaces between Serials Solutions and your website, or remove the name of a person who has left the employment of your institution.

Reports

You can also run reports in the Client Center, not just the overlap analysis. Previously, you could view the reports, but the only way to get the data out to work with it in a spreadsheet was to copy and paste, which was not practical for some reports running hundreds of pages. Now, you can export them into Excel and work with them as much as you want.

Problem Logs

Another place where e-resource information may be stored at your institution is in a problem log. You can have a web-based form for people to submit problems with electronic resources. Each problem submitted generates an e-mail to the electronic resource librarian, and it logs an entry on an online problem log. The electronic resources librarian can go to the log and update the problem to indicate it is "Under Review" or "Resolved" with a textbox to explain the situation. This is a great help in tracking problems and making sure they don't get forgotten, both for you and the person who reported the problem.

The log can also be used to spot trends if one product or vendor is having frequent problems. Some ERMs even incorporate this data into a built-in problem log.

Vendor Communication (E-mail, Phone, Paper)

Electronic resources librarians communicate with vendors almost constantly. You may send and receive an average of 50 e-mails a day, each way, as well as making and taking phone calls and opening U.S. mail. Most of this is from vendors, although some are from peers and colleagues both at your college and from other institutions. You will get advertisements for new products, notices about upgrades, downtimes, enhancements, new contents, and usage tips and offers. You may get sales calls from vendors with whom you don't currently do business as well as those with whom you do. You will get return calls on problem reports and pricing inquiries. Vendors will also contact you to set up in-person sales calls. Whenever a vendor tells you something that is really important on the phone, write it up in an e-mail to your boss or even to yourself immediately afterward so you have an accurate record of what was said. Eventually you will find yourself with many folders, each containing hundreds of messages. These will constitute the knowledge base for your everyday work.

Any time you need to see what was decided about an issue or when a vendor promised something, most of it will be right there in your e-mail files, carefully organized. Meaningful subject headings are extremely important for accessing this information later. Keep paper files with your legal documents, such as signed renewal commitments, licenses and contracts, membership agreements, and perhaps some invoices. You should consider saving more of these electronically when possible. Some print advertising materials may also be worth saving. If you bought a product on the understanding that it contains certain data as indicated in a flyer you received or that it has certain functionality as outlined in a note from your sales representative, save those. You will have these in case the delivered product does not live up to the promise.

Organizing communication is very important to the management and administration of e-resources. You'll want to find a way that works for you, and be sure to back up your files.

Websites: Vendors and Consortial Agents

Another source for product information is the websites of the vendors and consortial agents. When you are looking for pricing, start on these websites, and then follow-up with a sales representative if it says they'll give a price quote upon request. A lot of times you can get the information you need without having to wait for someone to put it together for you. The trouble here is that librarians have no control over when information may just disappear, and you can't very well save snapshots of vendor websites every time they change.

Here's an example of when we wish we had had this information. A predecessor purchased permanent access to a database on a vendor deal that promised an annual access fee of 5 percent of the purchase price in perpetuity. The details were outlined on the consortial agent's password-protected website. No paperwork was attached to the deal. We paid, they set up access, and ever since then, we have paid $325 a year. We are getting by on the honesty of the company, but should the issue ever come up, we'd be in a tight place because of having no record of the deal in writing. Unfortunately, the only place the details ever existed was on the WALDO website, and those details are long since gone now.

Meeting Minutes

Sometimes decisions are made in committee meetings or meetings with a boss or with a vendor. The minutes and notes from these meetings are more paper records of decisions and deals and are yet another source of information you need to save in your management of electronic resources.

Human Memory

Not to be overlooked as an important source for information not found anywhere else is the human memory, as the example with the $325 a year deal shows. Short of writing things down when you realize they are important, there's no other way to retrieve this information, but it remains an important asset.

Vendor Administrative Modules

As with Serials Solutions, many vendors have an administrative module for their customers. This is where you can see usage stats, change default settings, perhaps do some customization or branding. The features available will vary from vendor to vendor and product to product. It's worth exploring each when you subscribe to something new. Also, some ERMs will let you record what things you can do in the administrative modules along with the access URL, ID, and password, all in one place. You won't have to go digging around looking to see if you can change the default entry point from the basic to the advanced search screen, for example. When the vendors' websites get to be SUSHI-compliant and the ERMs add harvesting functionality as well, it'll be a lot easier to bring that important usage data into the system where the librarian can manipulate it in relation to other data, such as pricing.

ERMs

ERMs are billed as a single place to store and manage all kinds of information, everything related to the management of your institution's electronic resources. That's the dream and badly needed by the people trying to organize all the often-changing information in all those disparate formats and locations.

As a product in general, ERMs are maturing and improving, but their development lags behind the needs of the library community, so for the time being, there are still big gaps between the promise and the reality. One of the big gaps is getting data into them in a seamless, less painful manner. ERMs have a lot of promise; surely they will eventually fulfill the promise. Progress is being made, but they aren't quite there yet.

URMs

Unified (or Universal) Resource Management systems are the latest in development. As of this writing, none exist yet, but the idea is that they would replace the ILS and the ERM as a way to manage *everything*. From a meeting of the Ex Libris international users group, IGeLU, in September 2008:

> The underlying model for our Integrated Library Systems, such as Aleph and Voyager, is now more than 30 years old. While that model continues to serve libraries well in some aspects of their operations, in other ways it feels increasingly out-of-date. The library of 2008 is *dramatically*

different from that of 1978, and much of that difference comes from the explosive growth of digital information and services.

Given the level of change in recent years, it is not surprising that there are increasing tensions in our environment about the function and role of the ILS. After years of stagnation in the ILS world, suddenly there are talks and papers and projects all around us addressing the need for change. However, while the need for change is becoming widely recognized, it remains far from clear *what* new needs the systems that will replace the current ILS must address. We know the old model is inadequate, but we have yet to agree on what the new model should be.

From the document, "ILS—Next Generation/URM—Some Questions for Focus Group Discussions," used in the URM discussion group at IGeLU 2008 in Madrid.

An attendee of the ELUNA conference in Long Beach, California, in August 2008 described the situation at that time:

Ex Libris showcased the conceptual model of its current development product, Universal Resource Management (URM).

The URM is to be the next generation management tool for all library resources. Development will be multiphased. The first step, URM 1, will replace Verde as the Ex Libris electronic resource management product. Verde owners will have rights to the URM. It is slated for release Dec. 2009.

Ex Libris has no plans to discontinue development or support of ALEPH at this time. However, it seems the ultimate goal is for all library management modules rewritten as part of the URM. http://www.fcla.edu/eluna2008_files/eluna2008.htm.

As of the fall of 2010, planning is well underway, with an estimated general release in 2012.

At first, librarians tried to manage electronic resources using their existing ILS. But the ILS wasn't built to manage such complex creatures, and it fell short. So, ERMs were developed to manage the different-ness of e-resources. Now vendors are thinking of the URM. The trouble is, they haven't mastered the e-resource management part in the ERM yet, so we'll see if they are ready to integrate it all into one system. In the long run, one system makes a lot more sense, but first it would be better for the systems managing electronic resources to mature a bit more.

URM is still in development, although Ex Libris is working it through their think tank and has started testing with their development partners. A presentation of the product-in-development at ELUNA 2011 looked promising. It's still a year or so away, but it'll be the thing to watch as the next generation of resource management evolves.

SELECTED READINGS

Read at least two of these articles and answer the questions about them below.

Chisman, J., Matthews, G., & Brady, C. (2007). Electronic Resource Management. *The Serials Librarian, 52*(3/4), 297–303.

Miller, R. Acts of Vision: The Practice of Licensing. (2007). *Collection Management 32*(1/2), 173–90.

Skaggs, B. L., Poe, J. W., & Stevens, K. W. (2006). One-Stop Shopping: A Perspective on the Evolution of Electronic Resources Management. *International Digital Library Perspectives 22*(3) 192–206.

Stemper, J., & Barribeau, S. (2006). Perpetual Access to Electronic Journals: A Survey of One Academic Research Library's Licenses. *Library Resources & Technical Services 50*(2), 91–109.

THOUGHT PROVOKERS

Consider the following questions. Discuss them with colleagues if possible.

1. What are some lessons to take away from the Miller article? Are there any you could see applying in a practical fashion immediately if you were in an e-resources librarian position?
2. What is the difference between:
   —When a vendor offers a library the rights to the content of issues for which the library has already paid after the subscription has been canceled
   And
   —When a vendor offers a library "perpetual access" to that content?
   What are the implications of some of the various ways that vendors offer "perpetual access" to that content? What does the LOCKSS program offer to help ease some of these troubles?
3. What kind of information might be stored in each of the following: e-mails; spreadsheets; cataloging and acquisitions modules of the ILS; vendor and consortial websites; holdings management profile; library website and/or portal; proxy configuration information; administrative modules of the products; paper files with contracts, licenses, and other mailings from the vendors; plus what's in your own head. Can you think of other sources for information that should go into an ERM? If you ever have to set one up, this is a question the vendor will ask you as you plan the implementation.
4. Whenever anyone asks me, "What's the biggest issue facing libraries in the near future?" my answer is always "Interoperability." It's what stands in the way of federated searching being all that it could be; it's what is needed to make the seamless interface users expect, and lack of interoperability is the cause of at least half of my troubleshooting calls. What challenges do frequent new developments in technology (including Web 2.0) pose for the librarian trying to offer the kind of seamless integration of services our users expect? How does this question relate to ERMs?

CURRENT ARTICLE ASSIGNMENT

Locate and read an article on the topic of the administration of e-resources. The article should be no more than three years old and should not be one of those listed here. Write a one- or two-paragraph summary of the article, being sure to include the author's thesis, the author's conclusion, and your own reactions to the article.

ASSIGNMENT FOUR: LICENSES

Read and interpret several e-resource licenses to find answers to specific questions; gain a better understanding of the legal relationship of the library to those with whom the contract is made.

Read through two or three database licenses and one to two e-journal licenses if you can get access to any through your institution. If not, contact some vendors and ask for a standard license for a specific product. Read the whole license, then go back and try to answer as many of the following questions as you can:

- What conditions govern use by "walk-ins"? Are they allowed to use the resource? Under what conditions?
- What obligations are specified for the institution to control access to the resource?
- Is the institution allowed to send full-text articles from the database to requests for interlibrary loans at other institutions?
- If the institution cancels the subscription, will the institution retain rights to the content for the years for which the subscription was paid? If so, how is that continuing access to be achieved?
- What does the license specify will happen if one of the parties breaks the conditions of the license?

Write brief answers to the questions above for three different licenses, with at least one each being for a database and an e-journal/e-journal collection. You are encouraged to contact the vendor if you need clarification on any of the items above or if some of them don't appear in some licenses. These kinds of questions come up in the real world and electronic resource librarians will be expected to be able to find answers and make decisions without breaking contracts.

ADDITIONAL READING ON PROVIDING ADMINISTRATION OF E-RESOURCES

Clark, C. (2009). Shifting Sands: The Changing Landscape of Managing Electronic Resources. *Louisiana Libraries (Winter)*: 19–20.

Collins, Maria. (2009). Evolving Workflows: Knowing When To Hold 'Em, Knowing When to Fold 'Em. *The Serials Librarian, 57*, 261–71.

Ellis, L. A., Hartnett, J., & Waldman, M. (2008). Building Bearcat. *Library Journal (1976) Net Connect*, 6–8.

Emery, J. (2007). Ghosts in the Machine. *The Serials Librarian 51* (3): 201–8.

Feather, C. (2007). Electronic Resources Communications Management: A Strategy for Success. *Library Resources & Technical Services, 51*(3), 204–11, 228.

Fenton, E. G. (2008). Responding to the Preservation Challenge: Portico, An Electronic Archiving Service. *Journal of Library Administration, 48*(1), 31–40.

Liu, G. (2009). ERM System Implementation in a Consortium Environment. *Library Management, 30*(1/2), 35–43.

McElfresh, L. (2008). Standing at the Edge of ERMS. *Technicalities, 28*(1), 3–5.

Rolnik, Z., Lamoureux, S., & Smith, K. A. (2008). Alternatives to Licensing of E-Resources. *The Serials Librarian 54*(3), 281–87.

Ruth, L., & Collins, M. (2008). License Mapping for ERM Systems: Existing Practices and Initiatives for Support. *Serials Review, 34*(2), 137–43.

Yue, P. W., & Anderson, R. (2007). Capturing Electronic Journals Management in a Flowchart. The *Serials Librarian, 51*(3), 101–18.

5

Troubleshooting Electronic Resources

It would be difficult for someone to learn technical troubleshooting by reading a book. The best way to learn it is by doing it, repeatedly. Over time, you grow a mental library of things to try, but you will never master it entirely because there will always be some new challenge you've never seen before; but a few basic principles can be covered. Then you can look at some instructive examples.

Troubleshooting is much like the reference interview. It starts with a question or a report of a problem. Ninety-nine times out of one hundred, patrons will not provide the information you need in that first report. Patrons don't know what you need to know to solve their problem. They only know there is a problem they want solved. Most likely they won't be familiar with the right terminology. This doesn't mean they aren't bright, just that they have no need to know those words.

ELICITING INFORMATION

A troubleshooter must elicit the necessary information with patience and respect. This usually takes a series of back-and-forth discussions, asking questions, offering explanations, digging up details. Problem reports can come in many different ways, but unlike the reference interview, troubleshooting electronic resources in an academic setting seems to take place most often via e-mail. You may have the occasional phone call or every once in a while someone will walk into the library in person and report a problem to the reference desk. Then the reference librarian sends an e-mail to report the problem, and there you are again.

The good thing about an exchange via e-mail is that it provides a record of what's been said and tried as you move toward a solution, and also, if the problem comes up again, and you need to go back and see what you did before. The downside is that it can be fraught with the kind of miscommunication which happens too easily with non-face-to-face interactions.

UNDERSTAND THE PROBLEM

The first step is making sure you understand the problem. You will need a thorough and accurate description. Users will often just say "ARTstor isn't working!" or "I can't get in to ebrary." Get the person to give you a description of the problem in more thorough and clear detail. Explain that you need this information in order to correctly diagnose and solve the problem.

Here's a list of all the information you should get if you could have everything you want right up front:

- Patron's name and contact information, either e-mail or phone.
- What the patron was trying to access: the database as well as the author, title, volume, and date.
- Where the patron was working: on campus or remote and from which access point on the web page or was it typed in by hand?
- What is the patron's IP address: Send the patron to http://www.whatismyip.com
- Exactly what the patron was trying to do when the problem occurred
- The text of any error messages: perhaps even a screenshot

CHECK ACCESS

More often than not, problem reports come in overnight, so that you will often be seeing them first thing in the morning the next day. When that happens, it gives you a chance to do a little checking first before you contact the patron. If the problem description is clear or if it's a report of simple lack of access, check the access yourself. If you can get in, you can eliminate vendor problems and focus on the patron's setup. If you can't get in either, then you can start by contacting the vendor right away and skip many of the patron's questions.

SELF-CORRECTING PROBLEMS

Many times, the situation will have corrected itself overnight. If it is a simple access issue and you are able to get in the next morning, contact the patron and ask him or her to check again and let you know if it is still a problem. If you never hear back from the patron, consider the problem solved.

REPRODUCING THE PROBLEM

Checking access is one way of trying to reproduce the problem. For more complicated issues, you will still want to try to reproduce the problem. If the patron can't access a particular article in a database or is having trouble linking from one database to another, try to get all the bibliographic information as well as the exact steps the patron took, and then try it yourself. If you see the same problem, it's almost surely on the vendor's end. If you don't, focus more on the patron's location and setup. Trying to reproduce the problem is a very useful exercise in troubleshooting, especially if you end up talking to the vendor's tech support. Because you have experienced the problem yourself, you will be better able to provide the needed details.

SELF-HELP FOR PATRONS

Oftentimes, problems can be solved by simple things patrons can do themselves. Clearing the browser cache and/or rebooting the computer cures a lot of problems. When you've gathered the basic information from the patron, you can provide a list of things for him or her to try while waiting. This kind of information can be placed on a web page. Sometimes patrons will find the troubleshooting self-help page themselves and solve their own problems without ever needing to contact the librarian. Sometimes they will contact the reference desk. The staff working there will have been instructed to walk the patron through these steps first before passing on the problem to the electronic resource staff. Making basic do-it-yourself information available has been known to create a significant drop in the number of reported problems. At the same time, the problems that do come to the electronic resource staff will tend to be much more complex and in need of assistance to solve.

BROWSERS

In addition to cache clearing and "power cycling" (the term used to make turning off the computer and turning it back on again sound technically sophisticated), sometimes it is necessary to use a different browser. Like it or not, most interfaces for electronic resources are written for MS Internet Explorer (IE) and then adapted (or not!) for other browsers. So, IE works best for *most* databases, but here and there you'll find one that works better in some other browser. Making sure the patron has the most recent version of a browser can sometimes help. Often databases don't support old versions of browsers. On the other hand, if the most recent version is very new, there may be unexpected issues in trying to access an interface written for the older version. So, "Try a different browser" can be a good suggestion.

COOKIES AND POP-UPS

Many databases require the use of cookies or pop-ups. If these have been disallowed, the patron may not be able to use the resource. Usually those that require cookies or pop-ups will say so somewhere on their top page, but allowing them is another potential problem-solving strategy.

ACCELERATORS

One way that an accelerator increases the speed of Internet transactions is to bypass proxies. If your patrons are having trouble accessing a licensed resource from a remote location, bypassing the proxy won't work. They will need to find a way to disable the accelerator or at least the proxy-bypass part of it. Juno and Netzero are ISPs who provide an accelerator and oftentimes their customers aren't even aware of it.

FIREWALLS

One of the most common problems you may encounter is when a patron is at work at a remote site and trying to get into a database but is being stopped by the firewall settings at the place of employment. This often happens with students on internships or at summer jobs. If the use falls within the allowable parameters of your license, send the patron to the local systems administrator, because it is not something you can troubleshoot. If not, this is an opportunity for you to educate your patrons on appropriate use of your electronic resources.

DIAGNOSING THE CAUSE

Once you've gathered as much information as you can and have ascertained that the problem is not one of the simple fixes above, it's time to try to diagnose the cause. Troubleshooting is a combination of deductive thinking (eliminating possibilities), knowing how the underlying technology works so you can understand where things could go wrong, and often some trial and error testing of possible causes as you try to isolate the actual cause.

You've already started at the beginning with your users: what browsers they are using, which resources they are trying to access. Then you've got the IP address. Is it within the institution's range? If not, why not? Has the patron failed to go through the proxy? Why could that be? If a patron types in the direct URL, that will do it. As an example, a group of students were on campus trying to get into ARTstor. ARTstor was not recognizing them. Unbeknown to the electronic resources librarian, the students were typing in www.artstor.com directly into their browsers rather than using the link (with the proxy pre-pend) on the library page. Because the users didn't know about a change to the campus network that forced all users on campus or off to authenticate through the proxy, they were understandably bewildered as to why they couldn't get into ARTstor by bypassing the proxy and typing the address directly. As a troubleshooter, you must look for these important little details of which you and/or the users may not be immediately aware in order to solve certain problems.

POTENTIAL POINTS OF FAILURE

This book is not about network architecture, so it won't go deeply into the nitty-gritty of how every layer works. But the thing to do is to think through every potential point of failure, as many as you know, starting with the patron, the browser, the IP, the network (patron's, campus, vendor's), the services on campus (web page, URL link, proxy), the contract (Have you paid your invoice? Are certain use prohibitions enforced by the vendor's technology?), and on to the vendors: Is there a problem with linking? Is the trouble with the OpenURL, or do you have the wrong information in your holdings management service profile? Is there anything wrong or different with the vendors' servers? Is that one database the problem, or is it any database from that vendor? Or is it the specific resource being requested? Has an article been incorrectly indexed? (The test for this is to attempt to get at the resource using a search and then again drilling down from the volume, to the issue, to the page). Is it one of those pieces of full-text that is *not* in the database even though you'd think it would be? If a resource worked before and doesn't work now, tracking down a significant thing which has changed from then to now may provide a good clue. Drawing on everything you know about electronic resources and how they work, identify potential points of failure, and work to eliminate as many as you can so you can get down to possible causes. Once you form a few theories, follow-up with mini-tests to isolate and see if your theory may be correct or if it should be eliminated until you either determine the cause or have to go to someone else for help.

SCHEDULED DOWNTIMES

At about this point, you might want to double-check to be sure the problem didn't occur during a scheduled downtime for the vendor (or your institution, for that matter). Vendors will usually send out a notice, and they try to have their maintenance times in the wee hours of the morning when fewer users will be affected. If you suspect this may be the issue, find out from your patron *when* the problem occurred. If you didn't get a notice of a scheduled downtime, you might contact the vendor at this time.

TECH SUPPORT: ITS AND VENDORS

Even when you have lots of experience, you still often need to contact the vendor and/or your campus IT services for help in determining the cause of a technical problem with any certainty and sometimes also to solve the problem. Everyone wants the patrons to get to the materials they are seeking, so the tech support people are all your teammates in the troubleshooting game. Ironically, on many campuses, relations with IT can be delicate, and the people there, although they know more about how networks work than you could ever dream, often know very little about library resources and how they work. Unless the problem seems very likely to be caused by something on your own network, you may want to turn to the vendor first for assistance. Remember, they work daily with e-resources librarians and support people at libraries all over the country and the world. They understand library issues. They also may recognize the symptoms you describe immediately. They will have tech support people on hand whose job it is to help you solve these problems. Never hesitate to call upon them.

Multiple Vendors

When you start contacting vendors, here's something to keep in mind. Often there is more than one vendor involved, as the connection your patron is trying to make may very well pass through a couple of vendors on its way to its destination. Maybe a patron at home is using a local ISP to log in remotely through your campus proxy system to search in a Gale database, and then use an OpenURL link from your holdings management service to try to get to a resource in Elsevier's ScienceDirect published by Springer, but the link failed. That's five or six separate entities beyond the patron who might be involved: the local ISP, the campus IT (possibly also an additional support person in library systems), Gale, Serials Solutions, Elsevier, and Springer. In this case, chances are that if the patron got as far as Gale, it wasn't the local ISP or the campus IT. If the patron could get through Serials Solutions, but hit the wall at Elsevier, it *could* be the proxy configuration for Gale was okay but the one for Elsevier was not. Or that could be fine, but there was a problem with the OpenURL provided by Gale. Or there's no problem with Gale, but Springer provided faulty data to Elsevier when they loaded their contents into ScienceDirect; or Elsevier is to blame for not correctly indexing the Springer content or not handling Gale's Open URL correctly.

Finger Pointing

How do you sort this out? It may be tough because many of those vendors are going to want to blame each other. Well, that's unfair. In many situations, the vendor will find an error on their part, acknowledge it, and set about fixing it. But it is not uncommon for a vendor to take a quick look at the situation, see that another vendor is involved, and point a finger toward that vendor. Realistically, this is just a situation that comes up, and you have to work your way through it. Check and double-check and keep on checking with each party until you can eliminate all but one conclusively, and sometimes it won't be easy.

Solving the Problem

In the end, if all goes well, you will find the cause of the problem. Most of the time, once the cause is found, the solution is obvious. Maybe the user has to change browsers. Maybe you have to edit an entry in the proxy configuration. Perhaps a vendor has to correct an indexing error. However, there are times when there is no solution. Then you have to find a way to communicate this to the user with sympathy. Perhaps you had something entered in your Serials Solutions profile to which you no longer have access, or perhaps the vendor had given information to Serials Solutions indicating that the full-text was available for all of volume X, issue Y, of Journal Z, but, in fact, the publisher had failed to secure rights to three articles in that issue, one of which was the one your patron wanted. Your job then becomes one of communicating this to your patron in a tactful and sympathetic fashion. Whenever possible, offer an alternative. For the example above, you can direct the patron to interlibrary loan, and let your ILL people know that they should put the request through even though it would appear that your library has access to the requested item. But other times, there is no happy answer. Like any other unpleasant task, you still have to do it. You can express sympathy with the patron, but the bottom line is that the problem has no solution. How you convey that message is your own personal decision.

Problem Logs

One more useful tool for troubleshooting is a problem log. For example, Subjects-Plus, the free open-source product described in a previous chapter, comes with functionality to create a variety of web-based intake forms that output to an editable log, such as a problem log. Each reported problem generates an e-mail to the appropriate person and also shows up as an entry on the log with a status: Submitted, Under Review or Resolved. The report has a place for comments from the person responding to the problem report. That way, library staff can check to see if a problem has already been reported by someone else and what is the current status. It also provides a place to look back at previous problems, how they were solved, and if a similar one is reported weeks or months later.

Using a listserv is another way for reporting and tracking library tech problems. Patrons can send problems to this list, tech staff can monitor it, and respond as appropriate. An archive of the listserv messages serves as a problem log. This seems to be a better solution for a larger school with multiple libraries. At a much smaller school, the person doing the troubleshooting might keep a spreadsheet or a Word file, or an e-mail folder as a problem log—whatever adapts best to that person's work flow. But whatever the size of your troubleshooting workload, you'll be glad to have a log.

REAL-LIFE EXAMPLES

Load Balancing

A history faculty member reported she suddenly could not search in one of our subscription databases. She'd been doing research in this database all semester, but suddenly, although she could log in through the proxy, see the search screen, and enter a search, she could not get to the full-text for anything, even things she had been able to access before. A reference librarian confirmed that she had tried it and encountered the same problem. After getting the details above in real time, I tried and was able to reproduce the problem. That eliminated any problem on the patron end and shifted the troubleshooting focus to the vendor end. Looking closely at the URLs, it was apparent that each time a search was run, the domain name of the document was slightly different, each ending with a different number, whereas the log-in domain had no number at the end. The next step was to contact the vendor. In order to balance the load of traffic, the vendor had moved their content to various other servers, and none of the content was on the same server that did the authentication and had the welcome page. The vendor had thought this was just behind-the-scenes traffic management, but it meant that our proxy configuration, set up only to the one domain name we'd been given, was failing when it moved past the welcome screen to try to get to those other servers. We changed the proxy configuration entry for this database to include a wildcard character that would accommodate any of the various names the vendor gave their servers, and everything worked again.

Ebrary on a Power Mac

An eager-beaver incoming freshman sent a problem report in the summer before the fall classes started. Even with his log-in, he could not get the e-book reader software he needed to use to access a required text for his fall class to download and install on his new laptop. As time went on, more students reported the same problem with that e-book reader when paired with the same operating system the student had on his laptop. Although this sounds like the usual simple-problem report, it turned out that it took a *lot* of back and forth, trial and error, and eventually the involvement of the electronic resources librarian, the vendor, the library systems person, campus IT, their specialist for the operating system on the student's laptop, faculty in the student's department, *and* the original student who gamely agreed to work directly with the e-book vendor to solve the problem, which, by then, was also being reported by other customers. In the end, an incompatibility was discovered with the basic security settings of that operating system and the way the e-book reader had to be downloaded and installed. It required a somewhat tricky and complicated change of permissions in order for the user to change the settings that would allow the download, and also his browser had to be set to *not* allow Rosetta translator software.

This same semester we had learned that users of an image database using that same operating system *must* have Rosetta enabled or they couldn't use the image database. Any student who wanted to use both the image database *and* the e-book reader on the same laptop with that operating system had to have two different instances of the browser set up, one with Rosetta and one without. Neither a diagnosis of the problem nor its resolution would have been found without the help of all parties. In the end, the e-book vendor worked to find a solution and released a new version of their reader, which did not require this involved workaround.

The Incorrectly Indexed Article (Library as Correction Partner)

A faculty member reported that she had found a listing for an article she wanted in a particular database, but when she tried to display the article, it was a different article, nothing to do with her subject. I was immediately able to reproduce the problem, so I contacted the vendor. Their support people tracked down the problem and found that the article we wanted was on the same page in the print journal as the article which was displayed; someone had made a mistake in the scanning and indexing. The original article had accidentally never been scanned, even though it had been indexed, then incorrectly assigned to the scan for another article on the same page. The vendor reported the problem to the publisher, who had done the scanning (it was not done by the vendor), for correction. Meanwhile the article was obtained for the patron via inter-library loan. When it arrived, the article was a tiny little thing, a single paragraph, and not surprising it was overlooked by the scanner.

This example shows one of the ways that library users are partners with vendors to find errors, report them, and get them corrected. Vendors all practice careful checking of their indexing, but with such masses of data, small errors will creep in. Incorrectly indexed articles are not uncommon, but vendors will tell you they all appreciate hearing from their customers about the problems so they can be corrected.

SELECTED READINGS

Read at least two of these articles and answer the questions about them below.

Brown-Sica, M. (2008). Playing Tag in the Dark: Diagnosing Slowness in Library Response Time. *Information Technology and Libraries* 27(4), 29–32.
Donlan, Rebecca. (2008). Boulevard of Broken Links: Keeping Users Connected to E-Journal Content. *The Reference Librarian* 48(1), 99–104.

THOUGHT PROVOKERS

Consider the following questions. Discuss them with colleagues if possible.

1. What are some reasons for failed access to individual articles? How can those reasons be resolved? What can a librarian do to help prevent their failure in the first place?
2. What are some reasons for slow response times? What are some side effects for electronic re-source access? With whom might you work to resolve such problems?

CURRENT ARTICLE ASSIGNMENT

Locate and read one article on a subject within the general topic of supporting e-resources. Articles should be no more than three years old and should not be one of those listed here. Write up a one- to two-paragraph summary of the article, being sure to include the author's thesis, the author's conclusion, and your own reactions to the article.

ASSIGNMENT FIVE: TROUBLESHOOTING

Assessment of support problems using real-life examples: what you know, what you don't know, and with whom you need to consult to find a resolution.

Read through the real-life scenarios in Appendix D. Consider carefully what you know—and what you do not know—about electronic resources in general, as well as the one in question, and also about the specific example described. What questions do you need to ask to diagnose the problem? With whom do you need to consult to get those answers? What is a likely diagnosis, and how would you resolve it, if you can, from what you know? What would you say to the patron who is waiting for an answer?

Write up a one- to two-page report on your choice of three scenarios, taking care to address all the questions outlined above.

NOTE: This is a "cheater's assignment." You may call on the assistance of anyone you know so long as you indicate in your report which portions, if any, in your answers were assisted by someone else and by whom. In a real-life situation, you will run up against questions you cannot answer on your own, and it is a perfectly legitimate thing to do to call on a colleague for help. Try it out!

For your curiosity, some possible strategies as well as the outcomes of the actual problems, are described in Appendix G—but for your own sake, don't look at Appendix G until you have *finished* your assignment.

ADDITIONAL READING ON PROVIDING SUPPORT FOR E-RESOURCES

Chudnov, D. (2009). Practical Geek-Keeping, or, How to Hire—and Keep—Good Technical Staff. *Computers in Libraries, 29*(1), 25–26.

Dehmlow, M. (2009). The Ten Commandments of Interacting with Nontechnical People. *Information Technology and Libraries, 28*(2), 53–54.

Grensing-Pophal, L. (2009). Social Media Helps Out the Help Desk. *EContent, 32*(9), 36–41.

McCracken, P., & Arthur, M. A. (2009). KBART: Best Practices in Knowledge Base Data Transfer. *The Serials Librarian 56*(1), 230–35.

Hightower, B., Rawl, C., & Schutt, M. (2008). Collaborations for Delivering the Library to Students through WebCT. *Reference Services Review 35*(4), 541–51.

Resnick T., & Clark, D. (2009). Evolution of Electronic Resources Support: Is Virtual Reference the Answer? *Library Hi Tech, 27*(3), 357–71.

6

Evaluating Electronic Resources

TRIALS

Test Drive

A trial of a database is quite similar to test-driving a new car. While a webinar or demo allows the vendor to show off features, the trial lets you and your in-house experts try it for yourselves. During a demo, the searches will be canned, having been carefully selected and tested ahead of time to show off the best results flawlessly. Running your own searches puts you in the driver's seat. You can try your own searches and see what problems you run up against in real-world situations.

To Have or Have Not

The first decision regarding trials is whether or not to do a trial at all. You would think, sure, why not? It's free! It does take a little work to set it up and if it is going to be of any use, it will take time and effort. It will mean getting others to take time and effort as well to do some testing and evaluating, even before you come to making a purchase decision. You may decide to do a trial just to help stay aware of what kinds of products and functionality are available on the market, but do consider carefully before setting up a trial for a product you aren't seriously considering for purchase. It not only takes a lot of work, but it also can raise expectations in ways that become problematic if you decide not to make the purchase.

Whom to Include

One of the key factors in deciding to have a trial or not is related to whom to include in the trial. You have to decide to whom to give access, and that's where you have to really stop and think about it. The salespeople hope you will offer the trial as widely as possible, so users get hooked and press you to subscribe. If you don't think you'll really have the money, you might want to consider either limiting who gets access or not having a trial at all. Do you really want to create a demand for something when there is no money available to buy the product? Like anything else, look first to your institution's needs. If something is lacking in the collection and you have the money or you have the potential to cut something else to free up the money, then a trial is the thing to do. If you have a product and you aren't entirely happy with it and want to compare it against some other product, there's another good reason for a trial. You may even want to do two trials of similar products at the same time to compare one against the other; but always carefully consider the audience for the trial. You do not want to get people all excited about something they can't have.

On the other hand, some people may prefer to include the basic end user in trials, to see how they make out with the interface and if they find the product useful. One could potentially get some good feedback, as long as you have a way to manage expectations if you decide against the purchase after asking students to spend time doing a trial.

When to Have Trials

If you do decide to do a trial, the next question is When? You can do them ad hoc, whenever the issue comes up, or you can accept a trial when a vendor comes calling to offer one. This is probably the least efficient way. You can put all the trials off until the time when you would be making decisions about next year's subscriptions. A trial for a product about which a decision will not be made until a much later time is quickly forgotten. When it finally comes around to decision time, no one remembers the details of the trial. It's better to set up trials close to the time when a decision will be made.

Annual Trials

Doing trials of several products at the same time means you are able to evaluate them more efficiently and in comparison to each other as appropriate. You might set up a web page, perhaps on your intranet, with the basic information for six or seven trials or as many as you care to do all at once. You can include links to the trials, links to further information from the vendor of the product, IDs and passwords for accessing the trials, and the duration of the trials. You might consider providing an online evaluation form for your colleagues who will be making purchase recommendations. It need not be quite as full-blown as the "web-based evaluation tool" found in the Linberger, Fielding, and Bove article in the Selected Readings for this chapter. Remind all your colleagues participating in the trials as a group to have a look and do an evaluation. At the end of the period, review the evaluations, and consult with the expert parties who did the trials. With this valuable input and the amount of money you can afford to spend, you can make informed decisions.

While there may be times when an ad hoc trial is appropriate during the course of the year, for wholesale decision making, scheduling them all at once in the time shortly before those decisions have to be made is the most efficient. The timing of trials is a decision you should make based on meaningful criteria for your situation.

EVALUATIONS

Evaluating a product in a trial is where you put your collection development policy into action in a real-life situation. Each product should be considered against the criteria in your policy. However, criteria tend to be more general and say things like: "The interface should be user-friendly." But what makes an interface user-friendly? Those details are generally beyond the scope of a collection development policy document and will often change as new features become available and old ones become passé. You may wish to work with your selectors to set more specific criteria for evaluating trials, especially if you are reviewing any kind of specialized data, like images or streaming music, for example. Alternately, you can leave it entirely up to their expertise. The sample evaluation form found in Appendix E asks questions to get the selectors thinking about particular aspects of the product, such as the interface, the content, the currency, the ease of use, and so forth, with an open space for their comments to let them take it in any direction they like. Meanwhile, you will look at the pricing, the overlap with other products, the interoperability, the access method, and more technical features you will be asked to support, along with the license terms in case of any unacceptable conditions. Rather than reiterate the same criteria we've discussed before, you will find a sample evaluation in Appendix E.

Each institution will have its own arrangements for budgetary responsibility. Some will afford more responsibility to area specialists, some will give more to the electronic resources librarian, but most will give the ultimate responsibility to the head librarian. If you find yourself in a position to have some responsibility for such electronic resource purchase decisions, but not the ultimate responsibility, your goal with trials will be to provide the most relevant information to aid a sound decision, including thoughtful input from subject specialist selectors and reference librarians as appropriate.

You can get that input from formal trial evaluations, and you can also get it through informal conversations with selectors. You can employ the latter method if you are having trouble getting a selector to take the time to fill out the form. Either way, the basic information you want to assemble is the same. From area specialists, you will want to know: Does this product fit our needs, our collection, our mission and goals? Does it fill a gap in the collection or support a new program? The subject specialists will be the ones to answer questions about currency, authoritativeness, and appropriate content. Reference librarians will be the ones to answer questions about search features and user-friendliness. What worked well? What didn't? You, as the manager of electronic resources, will most likely be the person who needs to answer questions like: Is it a good value for the money? Will it work with the other services we already have in place? In addition to participating in the trial yourself, you will be asking the vendor any questions that arise as a result of the trial.

Evaluations after Purchase

As mentioned briefly in Chapter 2, every collection development policy should include a section on when and why to "deselect" a product, when to withdraw a purchased item, or when to cancel a subscription. Sometimes it is appropriate to reevaluate a resource on your roster to see if it is still up to snuff. In particular, when there is a big change, such as to price, content, or functionality, you may well want to closely consider dropping the product.

Red Flags

Here are some changes that should be alerts to an electronic resource librarian that a product should be reviewed:

1. A sudden jump in price: check the product against all your criteria to see if it is still worth the extra money or if you might start a subscription to something else that will cover that area just as well for less. Sounds like a good reason for a trial!

2. A change in interface that is getting a lot of negative feedback: vendors are constantly working to improve their interfaces and the features they offer. Generally these changes are for the better, although occasionally they will add something about which you don't care one way or the other. Every so often, a vendor will make a big change in the interface that your users hate. If there's a small change and your users don't like it, you can try contacting the vendor and giving them feedback. Maybe you can get them to give you the option of sticking with the old interface. When it's something major and the vendor is 100 percent behind the change, you can (and should!) still give them the feedback, but it may be time to start shopping for something else to fill the product's place.

3. Low usage statistics, particularly if the cost-to-use ratio is high: can you determine the reason usage is low? Does the product not meet the need you thought it would? Or is it a matter of your users not being aware of the product? Does it need better marketing? One way or another, it doesn't sound like you are using your fiscal resources efficiently, and it's either time to take action to get your product used more, or it may be time to consider spending your money on something else.

4. Loss of critical content: an important financial information product was on the market through an exclusive vendor for some years. Then the content provider's contract with the original vendor expired, and the provider decided not to renew. Instead, they decided to sell their content exclusively through another vendor. It was marketed as the same thing with a different interface; but upon closer inspection, the new version was lacking a piece of specific financial information that had prompted some institutions to subscribe to the product in the first place. When the new vendor was queried, it was discovered that the desired content was being made available only through that same vendor, but in an upgraded version that was much more expensive. Additionally, the new interface was viewed as not nearly as good. This situation left libraries with the uncomfortable choice of dropping that resource without any other replacement, but there was no point paying money for something that doesn't include any desired content that couldn't be had elsewhere for less. Many subscription databases are aggregated, which means there is no guarantee of which data you'll get to keep, but if the information your institution really needs is dropped, it's a good time to review for a retention decision.

5. Better products become available; one more reason to reconsider a subscription is if you hear of a new product that covers the same content and might be a better deal than the product you currently have. It's always a balancing act: chasing the best price can often mean changing the interface through which your users access specific information, and if you change it every year, it's going to be inconvenient and annoying for them. On occasion you may stay with a slightly more expensive deal just to avoid changing the user interface quite so often. If it were a significant savings, it would be more tempting to switch.

Evaluation Tools

Some libraries have developed "web-based evaluation tools" to help facilitate product trials. Some holdings management services also offer tools to aid comparisons and evaluations, such as Serials Solutions Overlap Analysis, which is a function in the Client Center when you purchase their 360 Core product. Scopus, from Elsevier, is primarily a citation database, but it also has backroom tools for measuring the impact of specific journals. For example: articles from which journals are most cited in other journals. Which journals include articles by the most-cited authors? From there, you can go to your holdings management service to see which databases have the largest number of these high-impact journals. These statistics help measure the extent of the influence of a particular journal, and in turn, the quality of the content in specific databases—all of which can help you decide how to use your e-resource dollars most efficiently.

A few free online evaluation tools are available as well. One is CUFTS Resource Comparison: http://cufts2.lib.sfu.ca/MaintTool/public/compare. It allows you to choose up to four electronic resources and compare how much coverage is duplicated between them. JISC offers quite a few tools including comparisons for e-journals, databases, and e-books. Their Academic Database Assessment Tool is at: http://www.jisc-adat.com/adat/home.pl. Statistics and User Feedback are additional evaluation tools.

USAGE STATISTICS AND THEIR APPLICATIONS

Usage statistics are a valuable tool for assessing the performance of electronic resources. Low usage can be an indicator for librarians to take a closer look at a particular resource, but retention decisions should not be made solely on usage stats. Many other factors may come into play. Usage may be low because patrons are not aware of the resource and what it needs is better marketing or more prominent placement on your e-resource portal. Usage may be low because, although the resource has high-quality content, the interface is complex or difficult to learn, or it may require a tricky download and installation of helper software. In this case, what it may need is more user training and support and possibly also a call to the vendor to talk to them about making their interface more user friendly. It may be that the resource was purchased for a small, specialized user group on campus, and the numbers you are seeing are good given the small number of active users.

Usage may also be low because your users don't have a strong need for the content, or they are getting it elsewhere. In this case, it's time to consider dropping the subscription and putting your e-resources money to better use on some other product.

Cost Per Use

Pairing usage statistics with cost information gives another useful view of your products. Divide your annual cost by the number of searches or full-text downloads per year and you'll get a "cost per" amount. Again, be careful to consider other factors before jumping to conclusions. High usage is always a good sign. Paired with a low or moderate cost and you'd automatically think you are getting your money's worth, but you should still take your subject specialists' opinions on the quality of the content into account. If you have lots of users using an inexpensive database that is packed with popular magazine articles and you start getting complaints from faculty about the quality of resources students are citing in their papers, that's not a very good use of your money.

On the other hand, if you have high use with an even higher cost, such that your cost-per-search or cost-per-download seems ridiculously expensive but the content is of the highest quality and you know you can't get it elsewhere plus the interface is top-notch, you are probably talking about ScienceDirect. You may find that exclusive, high-quality content that meets your particular users' needs together with a solid interface are worth the higher price, as long as your institution has the money.

What to Count

Searches are the most basic unit to count when looking at usage statistics, but they are only one of several kinds of usage statistics you may encounter. The number of full-text downloads is another commonly tracked measure of use. Some librarians count sessions, length of session, and turnaways. Length of session, for example, may be a useful statistic for a database offering streaming music or video. Turnaways are important for any database that has limited simultaneous users. A turnaway is when all the simultaneous users are taken. If another user tries to log in and is turned away, it is because the maximum number of users allowed has been exceeded. If you are regularly seeing a lot of turnaways, it means you haven't purchased a subscription to enough simultaneous user slots to meet your needs, and you should consider investing in more. If you see short, specific periods of time when there are turnaways, you may have the liaison to the faculty in that area inquire if they have an assignment for which it would be helpful if they had unlimited users for a short time, say, 24 hours. Most vendors are very willing to temporarily open up access this way if you just ask. You will have to consider what is most useful for you to track, and balance it against the staff time to manipulate and interpret the information you find. Dealing with statistics can be a time-consuming task, so be sure you are putting them to good use and not just gathering them and then doing nothing with them.

How Statistics Get Counted

For years, vendors decided for themselves what they would count and how they would count. Even though vendors A, B, and C were all counting "Searches," you might end up trying to compare apples, oranges, and kumquats, if you lined them up against each other. For example, when Vendor A's default interface searched across all of their databases to which you subscribe, users may not notice or stop to select only the ones they want even though they meant to only search Database X. They will have just performed a search in multiple databases. Vendor A would count that one search action by the user once for *each* database, in effect multiplying a single search action by the number of databases across which that search was run, leading to terrifically inflated usage numbers. They do also provide a de-duped statistic that counts only the number of times the "Search" button was clicked, but that statistic is for all the databases together, since they have no way of knowing which one the user might have wanted to search alone. Even aside from that glaringly obvious example, there are also slight variations in each vendor's definition of a "search."

Standards: COUNTER

COUNTER is a standard for usage statistics developed to address just this problem. COUNTER provides several different reports including:

- Journal Report 1: Successful Full-Text Requests by Month and Journal
- Journal Report 2: Turnaways by Month and Journal
- Database Report 1: Total Searches and Sessions by Month and Database
- Database Report 2: Turnaways by Month and Database
- Database Report 3: Total Searches and Sessions by Month and Service

COUNTER provides other reports as well; you'll have to look at the COUNTER website to see the definitions and updates, including provisions for the changes brought about by federated searching. A set of specialized statistic reports for consortia are found in the most recent version of the standard. For more detailed information on the COUNTER standard, see their website at: http://www.projectcounter.org/.

As with any standard, how the vendor implements it will vary, and although most vendors now claim "COUNTER-compliance," there are still vendors who don't. Those who do make the claim must stay within certain parameters to be allowed to call their statistics "COUNTER-compliant," but there is still leeway in terms of how that is accomplished. As of early 2011, Vendor A in the example above is still counting aggregated statistics because of the way their system is set up, so there's no real way to sort them out any better. So, now instead of comparing apples and oranges, we are comparing Empire with Cortland apples, and it's close enough to be useful information. COUNTER has been a very important step in making usage statistics truly useful and relatively comparable.

Gathering Information

Until very recently, usage statistics had to be gathered by hand. Some vendors would put you on a mailing list and send them to you in HTML, Excel, CSV (comma-delimited), plain text, or other formats. Some would include access to usage information within the administrative module for their resources. Some could be downloaded, while others you could only copy and paste. Some would post usage information once a month, some more punctually than others, with some being notoriously late every month and others reliably spot-on-time. Some offered the ability to generate custom usage reports, with the library administrator selecting date ranges, which products, what kind of stats, and so forth. Some vendors you had to contact and request statistics, then wait for them to generate a report that might take a few hours or a few weeks, depending on the vendor. Someone at the library, a librarian, support staff member, or more sensibly, a student assistant, had to spend hours each month, logging into vendor websites, downloading or copying statistics, pulling the information out of e-mails, or otherwise manually gathering the information and loading it into a spreadsheet or ERM.

SUSHI

Then NISO passed the Standardized Usage Statistics Harvesting Initiative (SUSHI) protocol (Z39.93). This is a protocol that allows COUNTER statistical information to be gathered ("harvested") by an automated program, rather than by hand. According to the NISO website:

(ANSI/NISO Z39.93-2007) defines an automated request and response model for the harvesting of electronic resource usage data utilizing a Web services framework." (http://www.niso.org/workrooms/sushi)

Because it is still new, only some vendors are "SUSHI-compliant," but that number should increase as more programs are being set up to receive SUSHI-gathered COUNTER information. Little by little, libraries can automate the labor-intensive chore of pulling usage statistics into their local programs for analysis.

Patterns and Trends

Another use for all those statistics you gather, whether by hand or using SUSHI, is trend analysis and patterns. Once you build up a year or two's worth of data, you can watch the ebb and flow of heavier and lighter usage, compare the rise and fall of one database compared to another, and try to sort out "why" and "What does this mean to us?"

If you track the usage trend for electronic resources at an academic institution, you'll find it follows a distinctive pattern. On a line graph, you will find two swelling bell curves with a steep cleft of low-use time over the winter holiday break. By graphing the usage, you will be able to see, plainly and visually, that the heaviest times of use are late October to early November in the fall semester and all of April in the spring semester. The spring swell tends to be greater than the fall swell, as graduating seniors get serious about completing projects they need to graduate. Institutions with vigorous summer sessions may see additional fluctuations from June through August, but on the whole, you'll find this curve holds true for most schools. This information is handy to know when planning how much time you may need to do troubleshooting, for example. More use translates into more support, so you can plan on those two periods to be busier ones, especially if the spring period coincides with a time when budget and purchase decisions for the next year are being made.

User Feedback: Random

Usage statistics are not the only kind of data and information you can gather regarding the performance of your electronic resources. User feedback, while less systematic, can be very useful for identifying issues that may need attention. Some feedback may be random, an unsolicited complaint or compliment. Take such information seriously as someone was motivated to take the initiative to give you this opinion. Just keep it in proportion, because it's the opinion of just one person. If you had complaints from several users or from faculty in the subject area covered by the resource or if you only heard from a liaison who was passing on several complaints or compliments, then it definitely deserves some more in-depth scrutiny.

User Feedback: Solicited

User feedback can also be targeted. You can offer a place on your home page where anyone can write in about anything related to the library. When you get questions, complaints, or compliments, it's routed to the appropriate person for a response. This is one way you can solicit feedback from users, and you will find you get a greater response here than you might have thought. It does not, however, solicit feedback specific to electronic resources. You have many ways you might use to solicit more specific feedback on a given electronic resource, but you will get a much better response if you offer treats or a prize for participation. Take information gleaned this way with a grain of salt, but it might steer you in a direction to investigate more closely.

User Feedback: Surveys

A more formal way to solicit user feedback is via a survey. With a survey, you can carefully craft the kinds of answers you are seeking. You still have the issue of getting sufficient response, but you also have a variety of options for the venue of your survey. SurveyMonkey (http://www.surveymonkey.com/) is very popular. A survey tool geared especially toward libraries is Measuring the Impact of Networked Electronic Services (MINES) (http://www.arl.org/stats/initiatives/mines/index.shtml). In the left-side navigation bar, you can see some other possible sources for assessment input. LibQual, or e-metrics, additional measurement tools, also have good reputations. You must keep in mind that survey information has its own strengths and weaknesses: a major strength is the detailed information you can potentially get from each respondent, the major weakness is that it can be very difficult to get a statistically representative sampling of respondents. Survey information, together with usage statistics as complimentary data sources, should draw you a more complete picture of the use of your resources.

USABILITY STUDIES

A more controlled way to gather information on the effectiveness of the resources you offer can be obtained through the use of usability studies. The details of how to construct and carry out a usability study is well beyond the scope of this book, but one can imagine any number of ways the information obtained from such a study could be useful in making retention decisions, in improving the way your library provides access to electronic resources, or any other library service, including problem reporting, or even for input to pass on to vendors on what features need enhancement.

ANTHROPOLOGISTS

A very new phenomenon in libraries, the anthropologist, deserves a brief mention. The University of Rochester, in Rochester, NY, has a resident library anthropologist on staff to help them better understand library user behavior.

To quote her: "If you have been making a bunch of assumptions based on out-of-date information, maybe it's time to ask some people some questions."

In the *Chronicle of Higher Education*, Nancy Fried Foster, an anthropologist on the staff of Rush Rhees Library, explores how undergraduates and others use the library and its resources. (http://www.rochester.edu/pr/Review/V70N2/inreview03.html)

If you're interested in learning a bit more about this very interesting experiment, you might start here: http://www.libraryjournal.com/article/CA6495191.html.

THE GOAL

When evaluating and monitoring electronic resource usage, always keep seeking new and improved ways to get a better and more complete picture. The goal is to get the most and best resources for your money in order to better serve your patrons and their needs.

SELECTED READINGS

Read at least two of these articles and answer the questions about them below.

Blecic, D. D., Fiscella, J. B., & Wiberley, Jr., S. E. (2007) Measurement of Use of Electronic Resources: Advances in Use Statistics and Innovations in Resource Functionality. *College & Research Libraries. 68*(1), 26–44.
Linberger, P., Fielding, L. J., & Bove, F. J. (2007). Developing a Web-Based Evaluation Tool for Purchasing Electronic Resources: A Librarian-Faculty-Student Partnership. *Electronic Journal of Academic and Special Librarianship. 8*(3) 17.
Webster, Peter. (2006). Bit by Bit. *netConnect. 0.2006(2006)*, 16.
Yi, H., and Herlihy, C. S. (2007). Assessment of the Impact of an Open-URL Link Resolver. *New Library World, 108*(7/8), 317–331.

THOUGHT PROVOKERS

Consider the following questions. Discuss them with colleagues if possible.

1. Would you include faculty and students in e-resource trials? If so, would you include their participation in some trials and not others? How would you present the trials so as to keep user expectations realistic? Which group would be more accepting of a decision not to purchase a resource they found appealing?
2. California State University at San Marcos used statistical analysis of e-resource usage data to determine that implementing an OpenURL resolver had an interesting side effect—it increased the usage of certain databases. We have seen the same effect here at Ithaca College. Can you think of other factors that might increase usage, and how would you use statistical data to measure the change they caused, if any? How else might you use this kind of information to improve your return on investment?
3. How does federated search affect search statistics? What are some other new technologies that might affect what's counted and how? How could the standards be changed to account for these effects?
4. Aside from vendor-provided usage statistics, what other statistical data can be obtained pertaining to electronic resource usage? Where can you get it, and how can you use it?

CURRENT ARTICLE ASSIGNMENT

Locate and read an article on the topic of the evaluation of e-resources. The article should be no more than three years old and should not be one of those listed here. Write up a one- to two-paragraph summary of the article, being sure to include the author's thesis, the author's conclusion, and your own reactions to the article.

ASSIGNMENT SIX: TRIALS AND EVALUATIONS

Select an electronic resource product that is comparable to a product available at your institution or with which you are very familiar. Arrange a product trial of the comparable product; consider the positives and negatives of the product in the trial; make a retention decision based on all pertinent factors. Begin by contacting the vendor representative for a trial and to discuss the details of the product. Write up a two- to four-page comparison of the two products based on the criteria in your collection development policy (see Chapter 7 for details of the policy assignment). If possible, include usage data for the existing product. (You would have to contact the library at which it is offered to get this information.) Using all the relevant information, make a decision whether to retain the current product or to cancel that subscription and purchase the product from the trial. Be sure to justify your decision clearly in a way that would convince administrators that it is the right choice for your institution.

ADDITIONAL READING ON THE EVALUATION OF E-RESOURCES

Bhatt, J., & Denick, D. (2009). JISC's Academic Database Assessment Tool as a Collection Development and Management Tool for Bibliographic Databases. *Collection Management, 34*(3), 234–41.

Botero, C., Carrico, S., & Tennant, M. (2008). Using Comparative Online Journal Usage Studies to Assess the Big Deal. *Library Resources & Technical Services, 52*(2), 61–68.

Brinley, F., & Plum, T. (2006). Successful Web Survey Methodologies for Measuring the Impact of Networked Electronic Services. *IFLA Journal, 32*(1), 28–40.

Chisman, J. K. (2008). Electronic Resource Usage Data: Standards and Possibilities. *The Serials Librarian, 53*, 79–89.

Clark, C. (2009). Shifting Sands: The Changing Landscape of Managing Electronic Resources. *Louisiana Libraries, 71*(3), 19–20.

Deng, H. (2010). Emerging Patterns and Trends in Utilizing Electronic Resources in a Higher Education Environment: An Empirical Analysis. *New Library World, 111*(3/4), 87–103.

Jacso, P. (2009). Database Source Coverage: Hypes, Vital Signs and Reality Checks. *Online Information Review 33*(5), 997–1007.

Makri, S., Blandford, A., & Cox, A. (2008). Using Information Behaviors to Evaluate the Functionality and Usability of Electronic Resources: From Ellis' Model to Evaluation. *Journal of the American Society for Information Science and Technology 59*(14), 2244–67.

Mitchell, N., & Lorbeer, E. R. 2009. Building Relevant and Sustainable Collections. *The Serials Librarian, 57*(4), 327–33.

Morrisey, L. (2010). Data-Driven Decision Making in Electronic Collection Development. *Journal of Library Administration, 50*(30), 283–90.

Negrucci, T. (2008). E-Usage Data: The Basics. *Colorado Library 34*(1), 48–50.

Noh, Y. (2010). A Study on Developing Evaluation Criteria for Electronic Resources in Evaluation Indicators of Libraries. *Journal of Academic Librarianship, 36*(1), 41–52.

Paynter, Robin A. (2009) Commercial Library Decision Support Systems: An Analysis Based on Collection Managers' Needs. *Collection Management, 34*(1), 31–47.

Sanville, T. (2008). Do Economic Factors Really Matter in the Assessment and Retention of Electronic Resources Licensed at the Library Consortium Level? *Collection Management, 33*(1), 1–16.

7

Capstone Project

This assignment builds on the lessons you have learned in the first chapters of this book. Your best initial source for information for this project will be the collection development documents from other institutions. Locate several of these, read through them, and consider their merits. Your decisions regarding the criteria to use for this project should come from what you have learned so far in this book, reading the chapters, reading articles, and doing the assignments.

You may also wish to consult *Selecting and Managing Electronic Resources: A How-To-Do-It Manual for Librarians* by Vicki L. Gregory (New York: Neal-Shuman, 2006). It has a section outlining collection development documents you may find useful, but the project can be successfully and well-completed with or without the book.

Your document will focus on two of the three parts about which you read in Chapter Two. It will need the "Philosophy" and the "Policy" portions and should *not* include the "Procedures" portion. The key part of the "Policy" portion will be the criteria for selection and deselection. Ultimately, it will be up to you to decide how to structure your document.

Now you have covered the entire lifecycle of electronic resources, from selecting and acquiring them, to providing access and administering them, to supporting and troubleshooting problems, to evaluating them and making retention decisions. You've had the opportunity to work with vendors, librarians and other professionals to give you a taste of real life experience. In this project, you will put much of that learning into an action plan in the form of a document to guide the selection (and deselection) process. When this is complete, you should feel confident that you have the skills and knowledge to be prepared to seek a job as an electronic resources librarian. But what is the work really like? Would you enjoy it? How would you get such a job? In the next two chapters, we'll look at a "typical" day for someone working in the field, and then consider all the components of a successful job search.

8

A Day in the Life of an Electronic Resources Librarian

No "typical" day exists in the life of an electronic resources librarian. First, the job description varies greatly from one institution to another. The title is not always Electronic Resources Librarian. Quite often the duties are combined with something else: systems librarian, digital collections librarian, serials librarian, or even reference librarian. Sometimes the duties of managing electronic resources just fall to someone who was hired to do something else entirely. The best situation is when the electronic resource librarian can focus on managing electronic resources without having to squeeze in other duties as well, but be prepared for that not to be the case.

Another reason there is no such thing as a "typical" day for an e-resources librarian is that it's such a dynamic and changing field. You can be absolutely sure that if you stay in the same position for five years, the work you are doing in the future will be different from the work you are doing today.

The nature of the work is variable as well. One day will be breakneck speed all day, with troubleshooting, meetings, deadlines, urgent requests for information, and a flood of communications all needing responses, and the next day could just as easily be very quietly spent working on a long-term project and organizing and filing communications. You can have a map in your head of what you plan to do on any given day, but that could all fly out the window with a single phone call or a flurry of e-mails focusing your attention elsewhere right away.

The first thing you'll want to do each day is take stock of where you are, then check new information which has arrived overnight to see what new things you need to address. Your day as an electronic resources librarian might look like this:

While the computer boots up, you hang up your coat and make yourself a cup of tea before settling in to work. After logging in to the campus network, the first program you open each day is your scheduling software. This allows you to get an idea of the layout for your whole day: the times when you can expect to be able to work uninterrupted and other times you will have for doing shorter, less focused tasks. You make notes on your daily to-do list of any meetings that will require preparation. Today you may have a midday meeting with a vendor sales representative. You'll want to review any problems or inquiries you have for the vendor. Your afternoon is free, so you tentatively plan to work on a long-term project preparing a list of licenses requested by the college's legal counsel.

You look ahead over the rest of the week. Tomorrow you have a Serials Team meeting and you are the chair. You will need to send an e-mail checking with members of the team, asking if they have items they want on the agenda; after you have received this information, you will write it up and distribute it. A librarians' meeting is scheduled on Friday, and you make a note to mention to your colleagues that a biography database has dropped some add-on content, resulting in a decrease in price as well as a name change. This will free up enough money to put toward some other resource of their choosing, with the approval of the College Librarian. You would like them to think about what resources you should investigate for pricing and other details.

When you have oriented yourself this way, you open your e-mail. You delete any junk mail immediately. You read any general announcements. Serials Solutions is notifying customers of a planned downtime for maintenance overnight during the upcoming weekend. Given that it is taking place at a time when students are less likely to be doing research, you must decide if it is worth forwarding to your colleagues. It's not such a big deal that it needs to be placed on the web page as an announcement to all library patrons, but since it's getting to be April and students are pushing to finish assignments, it might be a good idea to give the reference librarians a heads-up. You compose a brief note: "I don't expect it to be an issue, but just FYI, Serials Solutions will be down for maintenance Sunday morning from 1-3 AM ET."

You file a couple of vendor sales announcements, read about a delay in the release of a new version of a platform and file that, and scan news of pending legislation at the state level. The governor is considering cuts to library funding, and it's an important issue. A bus is taking librarian advocates to the state capital in a week, but you will not be able to attend. You file the notice.

Announcements for a couple of conferences and webinars are posted. You would like to register for the webinar on emerging technologies in libraries, and you make a note of the dates for this year's ELUNA conference. You'll register for the webinar later today and for ELUNA closer to the date. You note both events in your scheduling software, send an e-mail to College Librarian for tentative approval and put them on your to-do list. You file the ELUNA announcement but keep the webinar e-mail in your inbox as a reminder to deal with it today.

Now you look over each remaining new e-mail to see which requires action, but before you can read any of them, the phone rings. A new professor of Studio Art needs to be granted instructor privileges in ARTstor. You take a moment to pull up this professor's password file, log into the ARTstor administrative site, find the professor's account and grant the privileges, taking a moment to drop this new client an e-mail to say that an e-mail confirmation from ARTstor is on its way very soon.

The next e-mail under consideration is a note from an area specialist librarian inquiring if the library could switch from using LinkOut as the link resolver for PubMed to a new product called Outside Tool. It will require some research and testing, so the Electronic Resources Libraran writes to this colleague that you will check into it when time allows. You make a note on your to-do list.

A colleague stops by your office to ask about the changes in access to the *New York Times*. A faculty member is not happy that the publisher of the *New York Times* is going to start charging to view the formerly free content of the paper online and wants to know if the library has an institutional subscription. There's an e-mail about the same subject among those in your inbox that you haven't read yet. You discuss the response with a colleague, and then look up in your knowledge base of filed e-mails a series correspondence from a couple of years back when a similar question came up. There you find details about the various versions of the *New York Times* to which the library has access. You also check the current offerings. Then you send the faculty member a note indicating that the library has access to current content in the *New York Times* through several aggregated databases, plus a subscription to the historical content from 1857 to 2007, but does not have one of the new individual subscriptions. You put another item on your to-do list to look into pricing options for current content for institutions, if such is even available.

Finally, you see that the inside sales representative from EBSCO has sent the pricing and purchase option information you requested for the Mental Measurements Yearbook (MMY). The College Librarian had stopped by your office yesterday to chat about possible uses for some of the money saved from the change in the biography database. You were considering using it to subscribe to the MMY and asked your assistant to get information to help you make an informed decision. The EBSCO representative indicates that there is a good consortial price through WALDO, so you forward the information to the College Librarian, then thank the EBSCO representative and say that we'll let them know what we decide about a possible purchase.

You check the clock. It's been a very busy morning, and you have just enough time to grab a bite to eat before the sales call from the ProQuest representative. While you are heating your lunch in the microwave, you check your physical mailbox. There's an invoice for two Gale Cengage subscriptions you recently renewed. One of them is the biography database. Some days it seems like there's no break in the action. While you eat your lunch at your desk, you pull up the spreadsheet of estimated prices for this year's e-resource subscriptions. You confirm that the expected price in the spreadsheet matches the invoice. You update the spreadsheet with the new name and insert a note about the changes. The price for the second database is slightly higher than the projected estimate, but less than $100 more, so it's close enough. You pass the invoice to your assistant to be paid. The assistant makes you aware of a credit that was supposed to have been applied but wasn't, and he indicates that this issue will be looked into and the correct amount will be paid.

While you finish your lunch, you read an article on the latest changes to e-book purchasing models that has librarians worried. The issue of publishers using the electronic format as an excuse to roll back First Sale and Fair Use privileges upon which libraries have relied for generations is of particular interest to you. If you had time, you would sign in to the online forum and post your views on the subject, which you do from time to time, but it's just not going to happen today. You do save a copy of the article for the file on e-book business models for your work as a member of the Ex Libris E-Book Management Focus Group. This issue may well be of interest to their Unified Resource Management system developers.

You walk out to the circulation area to let the supervisor there know that you are expecting a salesman to ask for you, and just as you arrive, the ProQuest representative comes in the door. You welcome your visitor and move back to your office. You let your assistant know that their guest has arrived. After exchanging pleasantries, the representative begins to ask questions about what is new or has changed since the last visit. Bringing them up to date on the status of the new platform, the representative checks to see if they have had any problems with their existing subscriptions, presents some information on new products, and makes a gentle pitch for a product you have considered before but decided not to purchase at that time. You note that while it sounds like a good product to meet the curricular needs for a new major, you are not sure the funding is going to be available, but if the vendor could follow up with an e-mail with the details and pricing, you will share it with the College Librarian. You tell him not to raise his hopes, but you will take the information and keep it on file. You've had this exchange before with this vendor; sometimes the college subscribes to the product, but usually they don't. A good vendor always mentions these opportunities. You share some humor about something posted on a Facebook page, shake hands, and say good-bye.

You sit down to check your e-mail and to-do list. You see a new e-mail about an all-campus meeting. You note it in your scheduling software and file the message. Things seem to be quieting down, so your turn to your to-do list. First, you see that no one has sent items for the Serials Team agenda, so you type up your items and e-mail the agenda to the team. You cross that off your list. The College Librarian has sent a one-line e-mail giving you permission to attend the webinar, so you register online using your corporate credit card. Then you find the forms you must fill out for the college and for the library. Sighing over all the bureaucracy, you complete the forms, print them, and send them off for signatures. You happily cross that off your list.

Another e-mail arrives. This one is from an alumnus who wants to know if he can have access to the college's electronic resources. You respond with a diplomatic e-mail explaining how most e-resource licenses do not allow anyone who does not have a college e-mail account to be an "authorized user." You direct the alumnus to a library web page that has a list of useful, free resources offered by the college and suggest he also check with his local public library to see what they offer. Even when you have to say "No" to a request, you try to end the interaction on a positive note, emphasizing what the library *can* do, not just what it can't.

The phone rings; it's the Life Sciences Librarian asking if there is money in the budget for an online subscription to a new environmental science journal. There isn't, but if another title that costs about the same could be cancelled, you suggest that the savings can be used to pay for the new journal. As a subject specialist, it is the Life Sciences Librarian's decision which titles should be kept or canceled, so pricing information is needed. You say that your assistant will look into that and get back with the information. You then delegate that work to your assistant and ask that you be copied on the e-mail when the information is found, so you can be aware of what's going on.

While you were on the phone with the Life Sciences Librarian, someone else has called and left a voice message. A colleague in Interlibrary Loan can't access an article requested by a patron even though Serials Solutions indicates we should have access. You call back and take down all the details needed for troubleshooting, telling your colleague that you will let her know as soon as you have more information. You start the troubleshooting by double-checking that Serials Solutions says the library should have access to that issue of that journal. With that confirmed, you try to access the article yourself, using the same search strategy described in the problem report. You run into the same error message. You try to access the article by drilling down from the title, to the volume, to the issue, to the article, but come up with the same negative result. Having confirmed there is a problem, the next step is to check the subscription.

Has it been paid and is the information in Serials Solutions accurate? You send an e-mail delegating the follow-up to your assistant who manages the e-journal accounts, thinking that you can finally turn your attention to your long-term project.

You open the spreadsheet of license information for the college counsel and pull out the next paper file from the cabinet containing hard copies of signed contracts and licenses. Just as you are about to settle in to reading the details and translating them into simple language for the fields in the spreadsheet, you see that the new e-mail indicator has popped up on your task bar. You check your mail, and there are four new messages. One is a vendor inviting you to lunch if you are going to be attending the Association of College and Research Libraries meeting. One is the Studio Art professor following up to say that the e-mail confirmation from ARTstor has not arrived. The third is a notification from the problem log. A faculty member needs to use a business database during a class this evening and can't access it. The final message is a notification with access information for a newly acquired e-book.

Faced with several demands on your time, you must prioritize the work to be done. Your to-do list still includes researching options for subscriptions to the *New York Times*, researching and implementing a change from LinkOut to Outside Tool for PubMed, continuing the ongoing work on the license spreadsheet, and backing up your e-mail. The new items include responding to the vendor representative about ACRL, following up with the Studio Arts professor, forwarding the new e-book access information to your assistant, and dealing with an urgent troubleshooting request. Clearly the last item is the top priority. The research on the *New York Times* and Outside Tool can wait, as can the license spreadsheet. The new e-book notification can be quickly delegated to your assistant. A quick one-line note to the vendor saying thank you but you won't be attending ACRL clears that out of your inbox. A few moments forwarding the Studio Art professor the ID and password that haven't yet arrived in a confirmation e-mail resolves that problem quickly as well, leaving all your attention for the urgent troubleshooting.

The rest of your afternoon is spent in intensive concentration on the business database access problem. It begins with contacting the faculty member for more details than the bare bones you received from the problem log. Your work involves a process of elimination coordinated with the library systems person, the campus Information Technology Services, the vendor, and the faculty member. You update the problem log to acknowledge that the issue is under review. A fair amount of trial and error, testing and retesting, and communicating with all the parties involved is required before the cause of the problem is pinpointed. It's an issue with the proxy configuration. It takes several tries before the correct tweak is found, and you can finally contact the faculty member with the happy news that the problem is solved. You update the problem log again, including details and indicating that the issue has been resolved.

Looking at the clock, you see that it's about 15 minutes until the end of your day. You decide you have just enough time to back-up your e-mail files. You put away the contract files and close the license spreadsheet. You quickly file your sent messages, trying to keep that box clear and your inbox under 20 items, and then start the backup. While the mail is copying, you take a few minutes to send an e-mail sharing the article you read at lunchtime with a colleague at another school and ask for her opinion. With all that done, you can go home for the day feeling satisfied with your accomplishments. Perhaps tomorrow will be a quiet day when you can spend time working on the license project, typing up notes from the Serials meeting, and handling any other small matters that may arise. Maybe you can even take a break and go for a brief walk on campus. It's supposed to be a sunny, warm spring day.

As you can tell from the narrative above, an electronic resources librarian needs to be a very organized person. So many things are always going on at once that it would be a mistake to rely on one's memory alone. Scheduling software and to-do lists are important tools for keeping track of meetings, chores, and obligations. Logs and e-mail files are tools that can serve as working archives when questions arise later down the road. You will need these tools in your daily work.

Electronic resource management also requires a fairly high amount of energy to accomplish the number of tasks to be done each day; a procrastinator will not succeed in this field. The products, services, and technologies involved in electronic resources are changing rapidly. Mergers and acquisitions of one vendor by another happen frequently and keep the library landscape shifting. It's a very fast-paced and exciting field, which means it requires a person who is organized, flexible, and motivated to keep apace.

9

Tips for Job Seekers

Aside from the knowledge and skills, what does it take to land a job as an electronic resources librarian?

START AT THE BEGINNING: WHAT DO YOU WANT TO DO?

Start with your own interests. Is this the kind of work you would love to do? Managing electronic resources is intense work, so you'll want to be sure you'll really enjoy it. Your true interest will show when you interview, so don't try to fake it. Also look into what the job requires. If you are reading this book and doing the assignments, you should have a very good idea what skills and knowledge are needed—and you'll be well on your way besides. But you'll also want to read job descriptions carefully because the duties assigned to such a position will vary from place to place. Make sure you feel like you are a good fit for the job.

LOOKING FOR JOB OPENINGS

Looking for work can be a full-time job in itself. Sometimes the hardest part is just finding jobs for which to apply. National searches for higher-level positions, often including electronic resources positions, can be found in print trade publications from the American Library Association (ALA), the Association of College and Research Libraries (ACRL), Library and Information Technology Association (LITA), and other professional organizations. The College & Research Libraries Newsletter from ACRL is a particularly good resource when seeking a library job in academia.

Jobs are still posted in local newspapers, but more and more, the best sources for job listings are online. Many library organizations post jobs online: ALA and ACRL share a job site (http://joblist.ala.org/), while LITA has its own site (http://www.ala.org/ala/mgrps/divs/lita/litaresources/litajobsite/litajobsite.cfm). Be sure to also check the online job postings for colleges and universities in your geographical area(s) of interest.

One of the best sources for library job postings is a state or regional library organization. There is no standard name for such organizations from state to state, so you may have to do some research to see what groups are available. In New York, there is the NY3Rs Association of nine 3Rs councils serving regional groupings of libraries. Additionally, state library associations will have links to regional library organizations within the state, some of which will also have job listings. In Illinois, for example, the Illinois Library Association has a Jobline (http://www.ila.org/jobline/jobline-of-illinois). In Florida, the Florida Department of State, Division of Library and Information Services hosts Florida Library Jobs, a service of the state library and archives of Florida (http://www.floridalibraryjobs.org/), with functionality to search for library jobs by region. The California Library Association has a job bank they call the CLA Career Mart (http://cla-net.org/jobbank.cfm). LISJobs.com has listings of library job sites by state, which will help you get at the regional approach to your job search (http://www.lisjobs.com/jobseekers/state.asp). Each state and region will have a different organizational structure, but these organizations are terrific resources for job-seeking librarians.

You can try the general job-seeking sites like Monster, The Ladder, or Career-Builder, but you will almost certainly have more luck with a service more focused on libraries or, at least, on higher education. The Chronicle of Higher Education carries job postings for academia (http://chronicle.com/section/Jobs/61/), or you may have some luck with services such as HigherEdJobs (http://www.higheredjobs.com/), Academic360 (http://www.academic360.com/), or the National Higher Education Recruitment Consortium (http://hercjobs.org/c/search.cfm?site_id=793). More and more library-specific job-search sites are appearing. In addition to LISJobs.com mentioned above, you might try Get Library Jobs (http://www.getlibraryjobs.com/), which includes job listings from other countries as well. Another popular site is Libgig.com, which also has international listings (http://www.libgig.com/). You can even look for work on Facebook—try "I Need a Library Job" (http://www.facebook.com/#!/pages/I-need-a-Library-job/125220477532213).

Some of these sites allow you to sign on to a listserv or sign up for various feeds to notify you of new postings instead of making you return to the sites over and over. All the same, you should look diligently and regularly to be sure you are finding all the right positions for which to apply.

Another approach is to identify schools of interest and to regularly search their online job postings, or check with their human resources department if they do not have an online recruitment system. If they do, you will need to create an account and log in and search regularly. It's well worth the time because when you find a job of interest, you will have to have an account to submit your application package through the system.

The final piece of the puzzle is people. Do not neglect networking with anyone and everyone as a source for information on job openings. Tell your family, tell your friends, tell your neighbors that you are looking for a job. If you are currently in a job, you may need to be a bit more discrete; just don't overlook or underestimate the value of word-of-mouth when job seeking. One useful way to network when seeking a job is to use social media. Facebook, My Space, and LinkedIn are all sites where you can connect with other people and let them know you are looking. LinkedIn, in particular, has a focus on work-related connections. But take care. Exposure is a double-edged sword if you are not careful. During the period of your job search, you need to be highly conscious of the image you present of yourself to the world at large. Don't post your more flamboyant or risqué adventures on Facebook. Look at it from the perspective of a prospective employer. If you are posting about professional issues, you give a positive impression as someone really interested in your field. If you post pictures of yourself partying with your friends, it's not going to make you look like the mature and responsible professional employers are going to want to hire.

Likewise, look at your e-mail address, your chat handles, and any avatars you use which could be visible to a prospective employer. It's best to use an e-mail address with just your first and last names. It won't do your image any good to reply to an invitation to a job interview from an e-mail address like rumpusguy@yahoo.com or hotstockings@gmail.com. Carefully consider how you appear to the world in all venues.

As an electronic resources librarian candidate, you will be expected to be reasonably technologically savvy and adept at operating in an online environment. As you can see, that's reflected even in the job search itself. You will look for work online, chances are good you will apply for jobs online, you will almost certainly exchange information with perspective employers online, and you should be prepared to do some research online as well.

DO YOUR HOMEWORK

Once you have identified some positions of interest, you'll want to give yourself an edge. Before just dashing off an application, research what the primary duties entail on the library's website, the job posting, the job description, or anywhere else you can learn about the job. What is the focus of the position? Is this a library noted for being on the cutting edge, so they'll want someone ready to implement new technologies? Has the school been in the news because of being in a rough financial patch, so they are looking for someone who is good at finding the best deals? Does the job description seem to emphasize access issues, so that you should be up on portals? Look for key-words or buzzwords that you can reflect back in your communications to let the search committee know you have knowledge, experience, or interest in the same areas they are seeking for this job.

If you like what you see in terms of the job, you should also research the school and the community. If you can't abide snow, there's no point applying for a position in Minnesota. If you love the bustle of a busy city, don't pursue a job in rural Kansas. Likewise, if you are an avid skier, maybe those jobs in Colorado are more appealing. But beyond the more obvious geographical regions that might affect where you want to live and work, take a look at the makeup of the community. Does it look like the kind of place where you'd be comfortable and fit in? Find out as much as you can about the mission of the institution as well and if the culture on campus suits you. Do you know someone who works there or went to school there? Drop a line and ask. Does their website highlight a new directive in sustainability which you find appealing? You might mention it during an interview and impress the committee that you are a match in more ways than just the job skills. Finding out as much as you can about the environment in which you might work is useful in two ways: it helps you find a comfortable, positive match for yourself, and it gives you a chance to show the search committee that you have done your homework and are serious about your interest.

APPLYING FOR POSITIONS

Many times job seekers will just send out masses of applications for any job for which they'd be even remotely qualified. In hard economic times, you have to expect to apply for a dozen jobs or more in order to have a chance at even one, but that doesn't mean you should be applying for positions for which you know you are not truly qualified. Anyone who has been on a search committee has seen plenty of boilerplate cover letters. You need not write the most original cover letter ever, but you will gain points for customizing each one individually, mentioning not just the name of the position and the name of the school, but referencing some details you've gleaned from the job description or showing that you've done your homework about the school or the community. You will not only lose points if you accidentally leave in text from another cover letter, which obviously doesn't apply to the job at hand, but your letter will probably go straight into the rejection pile. Imagine how the search committee views you if you write about how you always wanted to work at a community college in Texas when you are applying for a job at a four-year college in New York, but job applicants really do make such errors. Don't be one of them. If you find yourself sitting down to send out one application after another, proof each one very carefully.

Often you will be submitting your application online via a job recruitment system. Sometimes these systems have clumsy interfaces, and response times are notoriously slow across the board, but most also allow you to view confirmation of what you have submitted. However, before you submit anything, you'll want to review the procedure for deleting or updating materials you submit, in case you make an error and need to make a change. If you have difficulties, be sure to contact the appropriate person for assistance, usually someone in either human resources or information technology, although it might be someone in the library. Taking your time in advance will help prevent embarrassment down the line.

THE COVER LETTER

Your cover letter is the first impression the search committee will have of you. You want to make that impression a positive one, and it will be even better if you can make it a memorable one. The best thing you can do is to be sure you clearly and concisely highlight the ways in which your skills and experience are a perfect match for the job. Look over all the information you can find about the job, look for clues to what will most interest the committee, because the committee will be looking over all the applications they receive for clues if you are qualified, have the right skills, and understand what the job is about. It is surprising how many people apply for jobs that they have obviously misunderstood to be something else. Be sure you know what the job is and what you bring to the table to meet the needs of the position.

It may seem trivial in this day of brief, rapid, casual communications via cell phone and Twitter, but your spelling, grammar, and punctuation are very important in formal correspondence, such as cover letters and job applications. You show poor communication skills and lack of attention to detail when you allow errors to remain in your cover letter. It also conveys a message of disrespect. Uncorrected errors say, "I don't care enough about this job or the people doing the hiring to be bothered to proof my letter." If that's not the message you want to send, take the time to be sure you are presenting yourself as articulate and concerned with making the right impression. Make that all-important first impression a good one.

THE RESUME

Readers of resumes generally skim them first to get a general idea of the applicant's strengths. Is this person more experienced in reference or serials or some other area in the library? Has the person had much work in electronic resources? Beyond the obvious qualifications, like an MLS or MLIS from an ALA-accredited institution, which is standard for any academic library job search, does the person have the formal qualifications required for the job? Be sure you know what these qualifications are and that you have them before you waste the search committee's time—and your own. Unless the market changes radically, most professional position searches gather dozens of applications. Only one person will be hired, so the committee is faced with the task of weeding out the majority. If you haven't got even the required qualifications, your application will be headed to the rejection pile in a hurry.

If you have a very long list of qualifications, you might trim your resume or vita by shortening it or leaving out bits less relevant to the job for which you are applying. If your resume is short because you are a new librarian, you might include brief, concise descriptions of work-related experiences in which you can highlight specifically pertinent experience. If you've had an internship or done coursework that covered work with electronic resources in depth, you might put that on your resume, even though it's the sort of thing you'd leave off an application for a more general library position. Find ways to emphasize how your skills match the ones that are needed, but don't be dishonest about it. If you really don't know much about the subject, it will show in time.

It's also a very good idea to have your resume or vita available online. Not only does it make it easier for the search committee to have your vital professional information handy, it also allows you to continue to update your accomplishments even after you have turned in your application package. Furthermore, you can include a lot more detail in an online resume than you can in a print resume. With a print resume, you have to keep it from getting too long, which often means ruthlessly weeding out all but the very most pertinent bits. With an online resume, you can put the highlights on the top page with links to more details should the reader be interested. So, for example, you can indicate you got your MLS from Syracuse University's iSchool on the top page, but make it a clickable link to a page listing the individual courses you took. If the committee is interested enough to pursue you as a candidate, they may well find it useful to follow the link and get a better idea of your specific coursework—while that would be much too much information to put on a print resume. In this way, you can give an online resume more depth without sacrificing the quick scanability of the resume format.

REFERENCES

The last item in your application is references. Noting "References upon Request" at the end of your resume is perfectly acceptable, but you should have them lined up ahead of time all the same. As with any job, you should choose your references carefully. The golden reference is going to be someone with whom you worked in a job similar to the one for which you are applying. Chances are, however, if you are reading this book, you are less likely to have extensive experience in managing electronic resources already. What is most important is that you choose people who will be able to say positive things about you which are true. The more they know about your work, the better, so definitely choose a former colleague or supervisor over a neighbor or relative. Some applicants try to impress by scraping a thin acquaintance with someone well-known for a reference, but you will impress your prospective employer more if your references know you well enough to describe specific desirable skills and qualities. The prospective employer would much rather hear from your reference that you are diligent in your work or that you are very good at finding solutions, than to hear some meaningless general comments from someone who barely knows you.

Never offer up a reference in a job application without first confirming that the person is willing to be your reference. It's not only bad form, but it could lead to the person saying something untoward when called for your reference. The best thing to do is to contact your potential reference and ask if the person is willing to give you a reference for a specific job or a type of position. You might write or call and tell your reference that you are looking for work as an electronic resources librarian. When you have a specific position in mind, if you forward a copy of your resume, cover letter, and the job description to your reference, it makes it much easier for that person to respond well to a reference inquiry if you get the prospective employer's interest. Your reference may even ask to chat with you about specific things you'd like to have highlighted during the reference call—for example, an internship you did working on a project related to the implementation of an Electronic Resources Management system or work in a serials department where they handled both print and electronic journals. The more information you can give your reference about the job you are seeking, the more that person can help paint a positive image of you to the prospective employer. You should also be sure to thank that person for being willing to be your reference.

INTERVIEWING

Phone interviews can be tricky, particularly if the whole committee is on the other end of the line. It's better to use a landline than a cell phone if you can; you are less likely to lose the signal and be cut off. Make sure you have the phone number in advance if you are to make the call; make sure you are sitting by the phone a few minutes before the appointed time, waiting for it to ring if the committee is calling you. Tell family and friends not to call during that time so the committee doesn't get a busy signal. Make notes for yourself to keep track of who is who. Be prepared to speak a little more slowly and clearly than you might ordinarily, and don't be afraid to ask for a question or comment to be repeated if you couldn't hear it clearly. You lose the clues of visual presentation—facial expressions, body posture, and the like—over the phone, but remember, that's a difficulty for the people doing the interviewing as well. The key thing is to be able to answer all the questions intelligently. This is your first live opportunity to show off that you are the right person for this job as well as your first chance to explore whether the job and the people are right for you. This will be an opportunity for you to ask questions that show you are interested in the details of the job, the philosophy of the institution, and that you have really thought about living and working in this environment.

If you are selected to be interviewed on campus, work as cooperatively as you can to set the date. Sometimes a conflict can't be helped, but if you make it difficult to schedule your interview, it shows a lack of sufficient interest, whether that's really the case or not. If you will have to travel any distance, this is the time to check on the arrangements. Will the school pay for your accommodations or reimburse your travel? Is there a set dollar limit for your expenses? What is the procedure you need to follow to make it all come off smoothly? Making sure these details are covered makes a good impression that you are organized and detail-oriented and avoids negative impressions that could lead to unhappy misunderstandings after the interview.

Be punctual. It does not look good to be late to a job interview. On the other hand, if you arrive too early, take some time to walk around the library or the campus to get a feel for the place. Then you can present yourself for the interview at just the right time, a few minutes before you are scheduled to arrive. Presenting yourself too early may put the hiring committee in an awkward position, so try to time it just right.

Be polite, forthright, and confident, but not cocky. Aside from that, be yourself. You want to be hired as the person you truly are or someone will be unhappy down the road.

You want to dress appropriately. People who work in libraries tend to dress comfortably in what might be called a casual-professional style. For your interview, you may want to dress a little less casually, but don't feel you need to go stiffly conservative. It's better to err on the side of slightly more professional than slightly more casual, but on the whole, as long as you are neat and presentable, library people tend to be fairly tolerant of different tastes in attire. It won't help you decide what to wear to the interview, but once you get there, take a look at what other employees are wearing to see if you feel you'd fit in comfortably. If all the men are wearing ties and the women are all in skirt suits, while you'd rather come to work in sandals and shorts, it might not be a fit for you. The best places are where you see people dressed in a variety of styles, from suits to jeans, each according to the individual's style.

Unless you are using it for a direct comparison of two similar things, expunge the word "like" from your speaking vocabulary. Using "like" as a filler word will immediately mark you as someone less intelligent than you really are. It also makes you sound unprofessional, and it will irritate your listeners. If you are a person who regularly interjects "like" into your conversations, you may want to practice not saying it for a week ahead of an interview. As with the cover letter, your language skills affect how you are perceived, so use correct grammar, be polite and professional.

PRESENTATIONS

An on-campus interview for a position as an academic librarian will almost always include a presentation. You may be given a very specific topic, a broad general topic, or you may be left entirely to your own devices to come up with a topic. Reference librarians are sometimes asked to "teach" a bibliographic instruction session to an audience of librarians and library staff, but an electronic resources librarian is more likely to be asked to give a presentation on some trendy new topic or on a topic of current interest to the library. If you are given free reign, select a topic that is as close to the interests of the prospective employer as you can. There would be no harm in asking, perhaps during the telephone interview, about issues that the library is currently facing or if they are planning to implement a new service with which you would be involved if you are the successful candidate. Select a topic that will not only give you the opportunity to showcase your knowledge on a specific aspect of electronic resources, but also your ability to communicate ideas to an audience of varying degrees of understanding of electronic resource issues. You will also have to adapt your topic to the length of time you are given. If you only have 15 or 20 minutes, you will have to choose a much narrower topic than if you were given an hour to speak. Be sure to leave time at the end for questions and answers. This will be your chance to interact with other employees besides the search committee, as well as to show off your ability to respond on the fly. An electronic resources librarian is called upon to do a lot of communicating, within the library and externally, so you do need to bring those kinds of skills to the table.

If you are using visual aids, such as a PowerPoint slideshow, be sure to inquire about equipment and facilities before you arrive on the interview day. Also ask for a little time before your presentation to set things up and make sure they work. Have a back-up plan in case there is a technical snafu.

Bring bottled water or ask for water to be provided. If you find you don't need it, that's fine. But if your throat decides to suddenly go dry, you'll be very glad to have it available.

If you are a person who is nervous about public speaking, do consider joining Toastmasters International or any other local organization or program in which an individual may work to improve public speaking skills. Toastmasters provides a friendly, non-threatening, and supportive environment in which you can hone your skills and increase your confidence in public speaking, making such a membership very valuable to a professional librarian. It also gives you a practice audience who can give you helpful feedback on your presentation as you are preparing for your interview day. If you don't have time, or if such an organization is not available in your area, do make a point of practicing your speech out loud and timing it rather than going in cold to give it on the big day.

QUESTIONS AND ANSWERS

You can't do much to prepare in advance for the questions you will be asked in an interview. If you know your field, you should do fine. If you've done your homework finding out about the nature and duties of the particular job, learned a bit about the institution and its mission, perhaps asked a question or two of your own during the phone interview to get a handle on projects likely to come up, then you've done more than many other interviewees. Take questions in stride and try not to let anything rattle you. After all, an electronic resources librarian needs to be prepared to deal with the unexpected on a fairly frequent basis. Don't rush to answer a question; feel free to pause a moment to consider your reply before speaking. You may get some more general questions in addition to the job-specific questions. For example, if the position supervises other employees, you may be asked questions about your supervisory style. You may be asked questions about your philosophy and views of the profession. You may be asked to give your predictions for the future of electronic resources. You've either given these things thought before or you haven't, in which case, you pause to consider before speaking. If you feel yourself getting nervous, take a deep breath and exhale slowly. A slow deep breath not only helps calm your mind and body, but it also provides more oxygen. More oxygen helps you think more clearly and also helps steady your voice. It's a small trick, but it really works.

OTHER MEETINGS

During the course of the interview day for an academic librarian position, you may be asked to meet with other librarians, staff members, sometimes even faculty or other members of the college community. Use these meetings as an opportunity to learn more about the people with whom you may be working. Take interest in their questions and ask about their work and how it would interface with your own. Oftentimes, you will be taken to lunch, dinner, or for coffee while on campus. Use this time to chat more informally—remember, you are under the microscope for the rest of the day, so no one will hold it against you if you take a break in the intensity to talk about a hobby or interest outside work. You might ask about places to hike, bike, or go square dancing, if those are interests, or where's the best garden center, or if there are opportunities to volunteer in the community. You may chat about your partner or children and inquire about local schools. While you shouldn't let your hair down and completely and cheerily confess to past sins and failings, you can relax a little and show yourself to be human as well as professional, particularly during a shared meal.

WRAPPING UP THE DAY

The on-campus interview is a time to be especially courteous, and you should thank all parties who took time from their schedules to meet with you. This is also the time to inquire about their time frame. You cannot ask how many other candidates they are interviewing, much less who they are, but you can ask if the committee has a rough idea of when they will be making the decision. The reply will usually be something along the lines of: "We finish interviewing this week, and then we'll take a little time to review and make a decision. We hope to have someone in place by August 1st," for example. They should be able to give you a rough idea about when you should hear from them—or not.

POST-INTERVIEW

This is the most awkward time of the process for everyone involved. You are sitting at home on pins and needles awaiting what you hope will be a positive reply. You may be waiting for news from more than one interview, weighing the pros and cons of each job even though you haven't yet been offered either, trying to walk a tightrope line between the disparate schedules of each. There's no magic formula for getting through this time. Calling to inquire is inevitably awkward and should be avoided if possible. You may want to call to ask if a long time has gone by (a couple of months, in which case you'll be calling to confirm that you were not selected) or if you have had another offer in the interim but you are still interested in the job about which you have not yet heard. Most places will eventually let the candidates who were not selected know, but it can take some time. They have to make a decision, check references, make an offer, have the offer accepted, and negotiate a salary and start date before they make it official. If their top choice falls through anywhere along the line, they may make an offer to their second candidate, or they may start the whole process over from the very beginning. Once the candidate's acceptance is firm, only then do they send letters to the other candidates who did not get the job. The waiting can be the hardest part.

THE OFFER

If you are the chosen candidate for the job, you will get a phone call with a formal offer. You should be told the salary and details of the benefits, if these latter weren't already outlined to you during your on-campus interview, and you will discuss a start date. If you are happy with all that is offered, accept. You can celebrate as soon as you hang up. If anything in the offer is not to your liking, now is the time to say so.

Do you need more time to move? Ask if you can have a later start date. Is assistance available to help you move? It would have been better to have asked about its availability during the campus interview, but now would be the time to ask for the details. Is the salary not quite what you wanted? This issue is more difficult. If it really isn't acceptable, you need to say so, but be prepared that the institution may not be willing or able to give you more. If the figure is firm, they should say so and let you decide whether you can accept the job at the lower rate or not. On the other hand, they may have some wiggle room to offer a little more if they were really impressed and want you badly. This is always a gamble, and it will be your call if you want to run the risk. Asking for more money colors the employer's perspective of you, so take that into consideration when you decide to ask or not. If it is your first professional position, asking for more money is not advisable unless you really could not live on what is offered. You can also ask for a little time to consider the offer, but if you do, make it a very short time, no more than a day or two. Such a request will indicate that you have some doubts, so don't make it unless you really do have some concerns you want to think through or you have the good fortune to be in a position where you need to make a decision between more than one job offer. You need to know such a request will make the search committee a bit nervous, because they will be worrying that if you delay then decline the offer, their second candidate may have taken another job in the interim, and they'll be forced to start over from scratch. With a little better understanding of the process in advance, you should be well prepared to seek and land the good job as an electronic resource librarian for which you now have the knowledge and the skills.

Appendix A

Sample Collection Development Document

Below you will find a sample portion of a collection development document. Pay particular attention to the criteria for selection.

_____ College Library
Electronic Resources Collection Development Policy
2/2011

Collection Parameters

For the purposes of this policy, "Electronic Resources" are defined using the AACR2 definition for machine-readable data files: "a body of information coded by methods that require the use of a machine (typically a computer) for processing."

Electronic resources covered by this policy fall into the following categories:

1. **Bibliographic databases**: Electronic indexes and abstracts
2. **Full-Text/Image/Numeric databases**
3. **Combination databases**: Index/abstract with some full-text; generally packages indexing one set of titles and providing full-text to another set of titles, bundled by the provider
4. **E-Journals**: Full Text online individual journal titles
5. **E-Books:** Full Text online equivalents of print books, in collections, or individual titles, free, perpetually licensed or by subscription
6. **Hybrid services**: Combinations of any or all of the above, plus other services such as multimedia resources, e-books, directories, news feeds, web link lists, etc.
7. **Websites**

Selection Parameters

The same criteria apply to the selection of electronic resources as those outlined in the general content development policy. Additional criteria for electronic resources include: access, functionality/usability, interoperability, stability, archiving, documenta-tion, customer support, format appropriateness for the content. All electronic resources acquired by the Library must be accessible in the Library and, except when technically or contractually prohibited, also be remotely accessible through the Library's electronic systems (OPAC and/or web page).

General Selection Criteria

Enhancements: The item offers value-added enhancement(s) that make it preferable over other print or non-print equivalents. The convenience of online access is itself an enhancement, as is the greater flexibility of searching electronic resources.

Content: In addition to meeting the criteria outlined in the general collection development policy for content, full-text/numeric/image resources are preferable to bibliographic-only resources.

Equivalent information: Electronic versions of resources published in other formats should minimally contain equivalent content, including such things as illustrations, charts, tables, fig-ures, etc., as appropriate.

Currency: Content should be updated often enough to be useful.

Access/Technical Preferences:

- Available via the World Wide Web 24/7
- IP address recognition, no password required
- Platform-agnostic
- Browser-agnostic
- ADA-friendly
- No special additional software required
- User interface is already familiar to the _____ College community
- Administrative module available
- Customization of interface possible
- Usage statistics available, downloadable in multiple standard formats
- Accurate and up-to-date holdings information, downloadable in multiple standard formats
- OpenURL capable
- Unlimited simultaneous users preferable to single or limited simultaneous users.

Archival access: _____ College Library may purchase available backfiles of an electronic resource if affordable and deemed bibliographically essential for the collection. Adequate arrangements for continuing access to backfiles should be possible, when appropriate.

Interface Preferences:

- Resource name prominently displayed
- Intuitive search interface including prompts, menus, and browse functions
- Basic and advanced searching functionality
- Single-search access to the entire electronic resource
- Online tutorials
- Context-sensitive help
- Printing and downloading capabilities

Vendor Support Preferences:

- Reliability and stability established
- Continued product support through updates and/or new versions
- Customer support: Responsive, timely
- Notification of any changes: Timely
- Documentation: Clear and comprehensive
- Trial period available

Cost & Support Guidelines:

- Scope and usefulness of the content to the _____ College user community justifies the cost of the resource
- The cost of the resource is sustainable by the electronic resources budget for the foreseeable future.
- Maintenance support (i.e., the technology and staff to deliver and support the resource) is available at _____ College Library.

_____ College Library participates in a consortial purchase for a desired resource when the agreement provides a significant price advantage over the cost as an individual institution.

Electronic Books

The library acquires electronic books selectively. In general, the Library prefers print format to electronic format for individual monographic purchases. In subject areas where currency of information is paramount, electronic format may be preferred. When appropriate, the library provides duplicate access to material in print and electronic formats. Consideration is given to the degree of importance for permanent access to the information.

Electronic versions of books that accompany the purchase of the print version are generally not be added to the collection, and are not added if they require password access.

Electronic books available freely on the web are judiciously added to the collection with consideration given to how stable they are and how much maintenance they require across time.

In addition to the General Criteria for any electronic resource, the following additional criteria are considered in selecting e-books:

- Consistency with print version (complete text with all tables, graphics, etc.)
- Ability to download and print content (this may be limited in terms of how much can be downloaded/printed at a time).
- Enhanced contents and additional functionality (highlighting, margin notes, bookshelf-capable)
- Clearly understood rights to access to the book across time:
  —Subscriptions, with no rights after cancellation
  —Perpetual license, with a separate access fee after cancellation (if applicable)

—Perpetual license with access fee included
—Or any of the above with arrangements for continuing access to content after cancellation or if the company ceases to be able to provide access (for example, delivery of content in PDF, or through a different provider retaining the same contract)

Websites

Websites are reviewed before being added to the library's content. Accuracy, authority, currency, coverage, and appropriateness to the collection are the primary review factors, in addition to the reliability and stability of the website.

Downloadable Documents

_____ College Library does not purchase downloadable documents, which the College has to deliver via printing and binding in-house, or mounting and delivering access locally. Exceptions to this rule:

• When the document is deemed essential AND
• When no other alternative is available

   OR

• With the approval of the College Librarian on an ad hoc basis for special circumstances.

_____ College Library does not store electronic back-up copies of such documents but rather views any downloading of documents as a purchase method only. We will provide access to such documents after processing them into physical objects for circulation; we do not host or provide access to downloaded content electronically.

Collection Development

Liaison Librarians identify, evaluate, select, and deselect electronic resources, as well as participate in the planning of electronic collections.

The Electronic Resources Librarian facilitates the evaluation of resources by acting as a liaison to the providers of electronic resources, setting up trials and demos, and helping to gather basic product information, as well as managing the resources in the collection from ordering right on through the electronic resource life cycle (acquisition, provision of access, administration, provision of support, and monitoring and evaluation). The Electronic Resources Librarian also participates in all aspects of planning of electronic collections.

The Web Services Librarian develops and maintains the interface to the electronic collection as well as participating in the technical aspects of planning of electronic resource delivery.

The Electronic and Technical Services Librarian assists with the maintenance of electronic resource organization and delivery via the OPAC and also participates in the planning of electronic collections.

The Electronic Journal Coordinator assists in acquisition and maintenance of e-journals.

The Library Technology Specialist manages the configuration of the OPAC and the proxy server for access to electronic resources.

The College Librarian makes final purchase decisions, participates in all aspects of planning and determines the budget for electronic resources, as well as doing some evaluation and selection.

Collection Access

Electronic Resources are delivered through a locally customized research portal, alphabetically and by subject, as well as via the OPAC. The Web Services Librarian is responsible for the general development and maintenance of the portal. The Electronic Resources Librarian is responsible for maintenance of links and descriptive information of the subscription databases. Liaison Librarians are responsible for adding and maintaining entries for free resources and for assigning subject areas to subscription resources. Some resources are cataloged in the OPAC and some are not, according to a combination of applied criteria and discretion of Liaison Librarians. Individual e-journals may also be accessed via the "Journal List" interface.

Collection Maintenance

Identification, evaluation, selection, and collection of electronic resources are on going. Decisions are made for the selection and deselection of subscription databases and e-journals on an annual basis.

Deselection

Considerations which prompt review for deselecting an electronic resource:

- Significant price increases
- Low use
- Availability of alternative resources which better meet selection criteria
- Unfavorable changes in format interface and/or content

Removal

Cancellation of an electronic resource results in suppression/removal of the bibliographic record associated with the resource. Relevant information, such as cancellation date, cancellation initiate, and other pertinent information, are recorded on the suppressed bibliographic record for future reference. For these purposes, archival/perpetual access resources are defined as an active resource only when access possesses a fixed URL, or is held in a local _____ College server, backup, etc.

Top Level Organization: Requests that links to pages or documents appear/disappear from the top-level page (http://www.ithaca.edu/library/) should be submitted to the Web Librarian, who consults the Web Team before making changes.

Content Review: Content creators should review all pages for which they are responsible at least once every six months. This review should ensure that the information remains accurate, that all links still work, and they all still point to the appropriate resource.

Appendix B

License Template

Academic: single institution license V4.0 Oct 6 2009

THIS LICENSE IS AGREED the _____ day of _____ [20__]

between

[**FULL CONTRACTUAL NAME**] of [full address] ("the Publisher")

and

[**FULL CONTRACTUAL NAME**] of [full address] ("the Licensee")

WHEREAS the Publisher holds the rights granted under this License *and*

WHEREAS the Licensee desires to use the rights and the Publisher desires to grant to the Licensee the license to use the rights for the Fee, subject to the terms and conditions of this License.

IT IS AGREED AS FOLLOWS:

1. KEY DEFINITIONS

1.1 In this License, the following terms shall have the following meanings:

Authorized Users   Current members of the faculty and other staff of the Licensee (whether on a permanent, temporary, contract or visiting basis) and individuals who are currently studying at the Licensee's institution, who are permitted to access the Secure Network from within the Library Premises or from such other places where Authorized Users work or study (including but not limited to Authorized Users' offices and homes, halls of residence, and student dormitories) and who have been issued by the Licensee with a password or other authentication [together with other persons who are permitted to use the Licensee's library or information service and access the Secure Network but only from computer terminals within the Library Premises].

Commercial Use   Use for the purposes of monetary reward (whether by or for the Licensee or an Authorized User) by means of sale, resale, loan, transfer, hire, or other form of exploitation of the Licensed Materials. Neither recovery of direct costs by the Licensee from Authorized Users, nor use by the Licensee or by an Authorized User of the Licensed Materials in the course of research funded by a commercial organization, is deemed to be Commercial Use.

Course Packs   A collection or compilation of printed materials (e.g., book chapters, journal articles) assembled by members of staff of the Licensee for use by students in a class for the purposes of instruction.

Electronic Reserve   Electronic copies of materials (e.g., book chapters, journal articles) made and stored on the Secure Network by the Licensee for use by students in connection with specific courses of instruction offered by the Licensee to its students.

Fee   The Fee set out in Schedule 1 or in new Schedules to this License that may be agreed by the parties from time to time.

Library Premises   The physical premises of the library or libraries operated by the Licensee, as specified in Schedule 2.

Learning Object   A self-contained unit of learning, education, or training comprising information content, learning activities, and metadata designed to explain a stand-alone learning objective.

Licensed Materials   The electronic material as set out in Schedule 1 or in new Schedules to this License that may be agreed by the parties from time to time [including such ancillary materials that are owned or controlled by the Publisher and produced specifically to complement, supplement, and support the said electronic material or any part of the same including podcasts, data sets, blogs, images, music, games, tests, and quizzes].

Secure Network   A network (whether a standalone network or a virtual network within the Internet) that is only accessible to Authorized Users approved by the Licensee whose identity is authenticated at the time of log-in and periodically thereafter consistent with current best practice, and whose conduct is subject to regulation by the Licensee.

Server	The server, either the Publisher's server or a third party server designated by the Publisher, on which the Licensed Materials are mounted and may be accessed.
Subscription Period	That period nominally covered by the volumes and issues of the Licensed Material, regardless of the actual date of publication, being the period ending 31 December following the date of this License and each twelve-month period thereafter, unless otherwise specified in Schedule 1.
Text Mining	A machine process by which information may be derived by identifying patterns and trends within natural language through text categorisation, statistical pattern recognition, concept or sentiment extraction, and the association of natural language with indexing terms.
Virtual Learning Environment	A software system designed to manage and support teaching and learning in education, including systems variously referred to as Course Management Systems, Learning Management Systems, Learning Support Systems, Managed Learning Environments, and similar names.

2. AGREEMENT

2.1 The Publisher agrees to grant to the Licensee the non-exclusive and non-transferable right, throughout the world, to give Authorized Users access to the Licensed Materials via a Secure Network [for the purposes of research, teaching and private study], subject to the terms and conditions of this License, and the Licensee agrees to pay the Fee.

2.2 [This License shall commence at the beginning of the Subscription Period, for each of the Licensed Materials as set out in Schedule 1 or in new Schedules to this License that may be added subsequently; and shall automatically terminate at the end of the Subscription Period, unless the parties have previously agreed to renew it.]
or
[This License shall commence on [date] and shall remain in effect [until {date}] [for {three} years from that date, and shall continue thereafter to be in effect unless terminated by either party by six months written notice to the other.]

2.3 On termination of this License, the Publisher shall provide continuing access for Authorized Users to that part of the Licensed Materials which was published and paid for within the Subscription Period, either from the Server [or from the archive described in 7.4] or by supplying electronic files to the Licensee [subject to payment of such fees as the parties may agree] [except where such termination is due to a breach of the License by the Licensee which the Licensee has failed to remedy as provided in 10.1.1 and 10.1.3 of this License{in which case such continuing access shall be provided in respect of Licensed Materials published up to the date of such breach}].

3. USAGE RIGHTS

3.1 The Licensee, subject to clause 6 below, may:

    3.1.1 [Load the Licensed Materials on the Licensee's server on the Secure Network.]

    3.1.2 [Make such back-up copies of the Licensed Materials as are reasonably necessary.]

    3.1.3 Make such [temporary] local electronic copies [by means of cacheing {or mirrored storage}] of all or part of the Licensed Materials as are necessary solely to ensure efficient use by Authorized Users [and not to make available to Authorized Users duplicate copies of the Licensed Material].

    3.1.4 Allow Authorized Users to have access to the Licensed Materials from the Server via the Secure Network.

    3.1.5 Provide Authorized Users with integrated access and an integrated author, article title[, abstract] and keyword index to the Licensed Material and all other similar material licensed from other publishers.

    3.1.6 Provide single printed or electronic copies of single articles at the request of individual Authorized Users.

    3.1.7 Display, download, or print the Licensed Materials for the purpose of internal marketing or testing or for training Authorized Users or groups of Authorized Users.

3.2 Authorized Users may, in accordance with the copyright laws of [*jurisdiction*] and subject to clause 6 below:

    3.2.1 Search, view, retrieve, and display the Licensed Materials.

    3.2.2 Print a copy or download and save individual articles or items of the Licensed Materials for personal use.

    3.2.3 Use individual parts of the Licensed Materials within Learning Objects for the Licensee's teaching, learning, or training purposes.

    3.2.4 Use Text Mining technologies to derive information from the Licensed Materials.

    3.2.5 Distribute a copy of individual articles or items of the Licensed Materials in print or electronic form to other Authorized Users or to other individual scholars collaborating with Authorized Users but only for the purposes of research and private study[; for the avoidance of doubt, this sub-clause shall include the distribution of a copy for teaching purposes to each individual student Authorized User in a class at the Licensee's institution].

    3.2.6 Download a copy of individual articles or items of the Licensed Materials and share the same with Authorized Users or other individual scholars collaborating in a specific research project with such Authorized Users provided that it is held and accessibly within a closed network that is not accessible to any person not directly involved in such collaboration and provided that it is deleted from such network immediately upon completion of the collaboration.

3.3 [Nothing in this License shall in any way exclude, modify or affect any of the Licensee's rights under the Copyright Designs and Patents Act 1988 or any statutory instruments made thereunder or any amending legislation.]

    or

[Nothing in this License shall in any way exclude, modify or affect any of the Licensee's rights under Copyright Revision Act 1976 as amended subsequently provided that such rights are exercised in accordance with Section 108 of the Act and with the guidelines developed by the National Commission on New Technological Uses of Copyrighted Works (CONTU Guidelines) and published in U.S. Copyright Office Circular 21.]

or

[Nothing in this License shall in any way exclude, modify or affect any of the Licensee's statutory rights under the copyright laws of {*jurisdiction*}]

4. SUPPLY OF COPIES TO OTHER LIBRARIES

4.1 [The Licensee may, subject to clause 6 below, supply to an Authorized User of another library {within the same country as the Licensee}(whether by post or fax [or secure transmission, using Ariel or its equivalent, whereby the electronic file is deleted immediately after printing]), for the purposes of research or private study and not for Commercial Use, a single paper copy of an electronic original of an individual document being part of the Licensed Materials.]

or

[The Licensee may, subject to clause 6 below, supply to an Authorized User of another library {within the same country as the Licensee}a copy of an individual document being part of the Licensed Materials by post, fax or electronic transmission via the Internet or otherwise, for the purposes of research or private study and not for Commercial Use.]

or

[Notwithstanding the provisions of Clauses 3.1 and 3.3, it is understood and agreed that neither the Licensee nor Authorized Users may provide, by electronic means, to a user at another library a copy of any part of the Licensed Materials for research or private study or otherwise.]

5. COURSE PACKS AND ELECTRONIC RESERVE

5.1 [The Licensee may, subject to clause 6 below, incorporate parts of the Licensed Materials in printed Course Packs [and Electronic Reserve collections and in Virtual Learning Environments] for the use of Authorized Users in the course of instruction at the Licensee's institution, but not for Commercial Use. Each such item shall carry appropriate acknowledgement of the source, listing title and author of the extract, title and author of the work, and the publisher. Copies of such items shall be deleted by the Licensee when they are no longer used for such purpose. Course packs in non-electronic non-print perceptible form, such as audio or Braille, may also be offered to Authorized Users who, in the reasonable opinion of the Licensee, are visually impaired.]

or

[For the avoidance of doubt, the Licensee may not incorporate all or any part of the Licensed Materials in [Course Packs] [and] [Electronic Reserve collections or Virtual Learning Environments] without the prior written permission of the Publisher, which may set out further terms and conditions for such usage.]

6. PROHIBITED USES

6.1 Neither the Licensee nor Authorized Users may:

    6.1.1 remove or alter the authors' names or the Publisher's copyright notices or other means of identification or disclaimers as they appear in the Licensed Materials;

    6.1.2 systematically make print or electronic copies of multiple extracts or make multiple copies of any part of the Licensed Materials for any purpose other than expressly permitted by this License;

    6.1.3 prepare derivative works or download, mount, or distribute any part of the Licensed Material on any electronic system or network, including without limitation the Internet and the World Wide Web, other than the Secure Network, except where expressly permitted by this License under clause 3.2.6;

    6.1.4 reverse engineer, decompile, alter, abridge, or otherwise modify the Licensed Materials or any part of them for any purpose whatsoever, except as expressly provided in this License.

6.2 The Publisher's explicit written permission must be obtained in order to:

    6.2.1 use all or any part of the Licensed Materials for any Commercial Use;

    6.2.2 systematically distribute the whole or any part of the Licensed Materials to anyone other than Authorized Users;

    6.2.3 publish, distribute, or make available the Licensed Materials, works based on the Licensed Materials or works which combine them with any other material, other than as permitted in this License;

    6.2.4 alter, abridge, adapt, or modify the Licensed Materials, except to the extent necessary to make them perceptible on a computer screen to Authorized Users. For the avoidance of doubt, no alteration of the words or their order is permitted.

7. PUBLISHER'S UNDERTAKINGS

7.1 The Publisher warrants to the Licensee that the Licensed Materials used as contemplated by this License do not infringe the copyright or any other proprietary or intellectual property rights of any person. The Publisher shall indemnify and hold the Licensee harmless from and against any loss, damage, costs, liability, and expenses (including reasonable legal and professional fees) arising out of any legal action taken against the Licensee claiming actual or alleged infringement of such rights. This indemnity shall survive the termination of this License for any reason. This indemnity shall not apply if the Licensee has amended the Licensed Materials in any way not permitted by this License.

7.2 The Publisher shall:

    7.2.1 make the Licensed Materials available to the Licensee from the Server via the Internet access to which is authenticated by [Internet Protocol Address] [Athens] [Shibboleth] as specified in Schedule 1. The Publisher will notify the Licensee at least [ninety (90)] [sixty (60)] days in advance of any anticipated specification change applicable to the Licensed Materials. If the changes render the Licensed Materials less useful in a material respect to the Licensee, the Licensee may within thirty days of such notice treat such changes as a breach of this License under clause 10.1.2 and 10.4.

7.2.2 use reasonable endeavours to make available the electronic copy of each journal issue in the Licensed Materials [not less than {XX}days before the date] [not later than the day] of publication of the printed version. In the event that for technical reasons this is not possible for any particular journal, as a matter of course, such journal shall be identified at the time of licensing, together with such reasons.

7.2.3 provide the Licensee, within 30 days of the date of this License, with information sufficient to enable the Licensee to access the Licensed Material.

7.2.4 use reasonable endeavours to ensure that the Server has adequate capacity and bandwidth to support the usage of the Licensee at a level commensurate with the standards of availability for information services of similar scope operating via the World Wide Web, as such standards evolve from time to time over the term of this License.

7.2.5 use reasonable endeavours to make the Licensed Materials available to the Licensee and to Authorized Users at all times and on a twenty-four hour basis, save for routine maintenance (which shall be notified to the Licensee in advance wherever possible), and to restore access to the Licensed Materials as soon as possible in the event of an interruption or suspension of the service.

7.3 [Where the Licensed Materials shall not be available to the Licensee for more than thirty (30) consecutive days, the Publisher shall refund to the Licensee a proportion of the Fee prorated to the period of such unavailability within the Subscription Period to which the Fee relates.]

7.4 The Publisher reserves the right at any time to withdraw from the Licensed Materials any item or part of an item for which it no longer retains the right to publish, or which it has reasonable grounds to believe infringes copyright or is defamatory, obscene, unlawful, or otherwise objectionable. The Publisher shall give written notice to the Licensee of such withdrawal. If the withdrawal [represents more than ten per cent (10%) of the book, journal, or other publication in which it appeared, the Publisher shall refund to the Licensee that part of the Fee that is in proportion to the amount of material withdrawn and the remaining un-expired portion of the Subscription Period][results in the Licensed Materials being no longer useful to the Licensee, the Licensee may within thirty days of such notice treat such changes as a breach of this License under clause 10.1.2 and 10.4].

7.5 The Publisher undertakes to [use reasonable endeavours to] provide or to make arrangements for a third party to provide an archive of the Licensed Materials for the purposes of long-term preservation of the Licensed Materials and to permit Authorized Users to access such archive after termination of this License.]

7.6 Collection and analysis of data on the usage of the Licensed Materials will assist both the Publisher and the Licensee to understand the impact of this License. The Publisher shall provide to the Licensee or facilitate the collection and provision to the Licensee and the Publisher by the Licensee of such usage data on the number [of titles] [of abstracts and] of articles downloaded, by journal title, on [a monthly] [a quarterly][an annual] basis for the Publisher's and the Licensee's private internal use only. Such usage data shall be compiled in a manner consistent with applicable privacy [and data protection] laws [and as may be agreed between the parties from time to time], and the anonymity of individual users and the confidentiality of their searches shall be fully protected. In the case that the Publisher assigns its rights to another party under clause 11.3, the Licensee may at its discretion require the assignee either to keep such usage information confidential or to destroy it.

7.7 EXCEPT AS EXPRESSLY PROVIDED IN THIS LICENSE, THE PUBLISHER MAKES NO REPRESENTATIONS OR WARRANTIES OF ANY KIND, EXPRESS OR IMPLIED, INCLUDING, BUT NOT LIMITED TO, WARRANTIES OF DESIGN, ACCURACY OF THE INFORMATION CONTAINED IN THE LICENSED MATERIALS, MERCHANTABILITY OR FITNESS OF USE FOR A PARTICULAR PURPOSE. THE LICENSED MATERIALS ARE SUPPLIED 'AS IS'.

7.8 EXCEPT AS PROVIDED IN CLAUSE 7.1, UNDER NO CIRCUMSTANCES SHALL THE PUBLISHER BE LIABLE TO THE LICENSEE OR ANY OTHER PERSON, INCLUDING BUT NOT LIMITED TO AUTHORIZED USERS, FOR ANY SPECIAL, EXEMPLARY, INCIDENTAL OR CONSEQUENTIAL DAMAGES OF ANY CHARACTER ARISING OUT OF THE INABILITY TO USE, OR THE USE OF, THE LICENSED MATERIALS. IRRESPECTIVE OF THE CAUSE OR FORM OF ACTION, THE PUBLISHER'S AGGREGATE LIABILITY FOR ANY CLAIMS, LOSSES, OR DAMAGES ARISING OUT OF ANY BREACH OF THIS LICENSE SHALL IN NO CIRCUMSTANCES EXCEED THE FEE PAID BY LICENSEE TO THE PUBLISHER UNDER THIS LICENSE IN RESPECT OF THE SUBSCRIPTION PERIOD DURING WHICH SUCH CLAIM, LOSS OR DAMAGE OCCURRED. THE FOREGOING LIMITATION OF LIABILITY AND EXCLUSION OF CERTAIN DAMAGES SHALL APPLY REGARDLESS OF THE SUCCESS OR EFFECTIVENESS OF OTHER REMEDIES. [REGARDLESS OF THE CAUSE OR FORM OF ACTION, THE LICENSEE MAY BRING NO ACTION ARISING FROM THIS LICENSE MORE THAN [SIX (6)][TWELVE (12)] MONTHS AFTER THE CAUSE OF ACTION ARISES.]

8. LICENSEE'S UNDERTAKINGS

8.1 The Licensee shall:

8.1.1 use reasonable endeavours to ensure that all Authorized Users are aware of the importance of respecting the intellectual property rights in the Licensed Materials and of the terms and conditions of this License, and use reasonable endeavours to notify Authorized Users of the terms and conditions of this License and take steps to protect the Licensed Materials from unAuthorized use or other breach of this License;

8.1.2 use reasonable endeavours to monitor compliance and immediately upon becoming aware of any unAuthorized use or other breach, inform the Publisher and take all reasonable and appropriate steps, including disciplinary action, both to ensure that such activity ceases and to prevent any recurrence;

8.1.3 [issue passwords or other access information only to Authorized Users and use all reasonable endeavours to ensure that Authorized Users do not divulge their passwords or other access information to any third party;]

8.1.4 provide the Publisher, within 30 days of the date of this Agreement, with information sufficient to enable the Publisher to provide access to the Licensed Material in accordance with its obligation under clause 7.2.3. Should the Licensee make any significant change to such information, it will notify the Publisher not less than ten (10) days before the change takes effect.

8.1.5 keep full and up-to-date records of all [Authorized Users and their access details][IP addresses] and provide the Publisher with details of such additions, deletions or other alterations to such records as are necessary to enable the Publisher to provide Authorized Users with access to the Licensed Materials as contemplated by this License.

8.2 [{SUBJECT TO APPLICABLE LAW,}THE LICENSEE AGREES TO INDEMNIFY, DEFEND AND HOLD THE PUBLISHER HARMLESS FROM AND AGAINST ANY LOSS, DAMAGE, COSTS, LIABILITY AND EXPENSES (INCLUDING REASONABLE LEGAL AND PROFESSIONAL FEES) ARISING OUT OF ANY CLAIM OR LEGAL ACTION TAKEN AGAINST THE PUBLISHER RELATED TO OR IN ANY WAY CONNECTED WITH ANY USE OF THE LICENSED MATERIALS BY THE LICENSEE OR AUTHORIZED USERS OR ANY FAILURE BY THE LICENSEE TO PERFORM ITS OBLIGATIONS IN RELATION TO THIS LICENSE, PROVIDED THAT] NOTHING IN THIS LICENSE SHALL MAKE THE LICENSEE LIABLE FOR BREACH OF THE TERMS OF THE LICENSE BY ANY AUTHORIZED USER PROVIDED THAT THE LICENSEE DID NOT CAUSE, KNOWINGLY ASSIST OR CONDONE THE CONTINUATION OF SUCH BREACH TO CONTINUE AFTER BECOMING AWARE OF AN ACTUAL BREACH HAVING OCCURRED.

8.3 The Licensee shall, in consideration for the rights granted under this License, pay the Fee within [thirty (30)] [sixty (60)] days [of signature] [of receipt of invoice] and, if applicable, within [thirty (30)] [sixty (60)] days [of receipt of invoice relating to] [prior to] each subsequent Subscription Period[and receipt of such payment shall be a condition of this License coming into effect]. For the avoidance of doubt, the Fee shall be exclusive of any sales, use, value added, or similar taxes and the Licensee shall be liable for any such taxes in addition to the Fee.

9. UNDERTAKINGS BY BOTH PARTIES

9.1 Each party shall use its best endeavours to safeguard the intellectual property, confidential information and proprietary rights of the other party.

10. TERM AND TERMINATION

10.1 In addition to automatic termination (unless renewed) under clause 2.2, this License shall be terminated:

10.1.1 if the Licensee wilfully defaults in making payment of the Fee as provided in this License and fails to remedy such default within [thirty {30}] [sixty {60}] days of notification in writing by the Publisher;

10.1.2 if the Publisher commits a material or persistent breach of any term of this License and fails to remedy the breach (if capable of remedy) within [thirty {30}] [sixty {60}] days of notification in writing by the Licensee;

10.1.3 if the Licensee commits a wilful material and persistent breach of the Publisher's copyright or other intellectual property rights or of the provisions of clause 3 in respect of usage rights or of clause 6 in respect of prohibited uses;

10.1.4 if either party becomes insolvent or becomes subject to receivership, liquidation or similar external administration.

10.2 On termination all rights and obligations of the parties automatically terminate except for obligations in respect of Licensed Materials to which access continues to be permitted as provided in clause 2.3.

10.3 On termination of this License for cause, as specified in clauses 10.1.1 and 10.1.3, the Licensee shall immediately cease to distribute or make available the Licensed Materials to Authorized Users [and shall return to the Publisher or destroy all Licensed Materials locally mounted pursuant to clause 3.1.1 and 3.1.2] except as provided in clause 2.3.

10.4 On termination of this License by the Licensee for cause, as specified in clause 10.1.2 above, the Publisher shall forthwith refund the proportion of the Fee that represents the paid but un-expired part of the Subscription Period.

11. GENERAL

11.1 This License constitutes the entire agreement of the parties and supersedes all prior communications, understandings and agreements relating to the subject matter of this License, whether oral or written.

11.2 Alterations to this License and to the Schedules to this License are only valid if they are recorded in writing and signed by both parties.

11.3 This License may not be assigned by either party to any other person or organisation, nor may either party sub-contract any of its obligations, except as provided in this License in respect of the management and operation of the Server, without the prior written consent of the other party, which consent shall not unreasonably be withheld.

11.4 If rights in all or any part of the Licensed Materials are assigned to another publisher, the Publisher shall [use its best endeavours to] ensure that the terms and conditions of this License are maintained.

11.5 Any notices to be served on either of the parties by the other shall be sent by pre-paid recorded delivery or registered post to the address of the addressee as set out in this License or to such other address as notified by either party to the other as its address for service of notices. All such notices shall be deemed to have been received within 14 days of posting.

11.6 Neither party's delay or failure to perform any provision of this License, as result of circumstances beyond its control (including, without limitation, war, strikes, floods, governmental restrictions, power, telecommunications, or Internet failures, or damage to or destruction of any network facilities) shall be deemed to be, or to give rise to, a breach of this License.

11.7 The invalidity or un-enforceability of any provision of this License shall not affect the continuation or enforceability of the remainder of this License.

11.8 Either party's waiver, or failure to require performance by the other, of any provision of this License will not affect its full right to require such performance at any subsequent time, or be taken or held to be a waiver of the provision itself.

11.9 [This License shall be governed by and construed in accordance with {*jurisdiction*} law; the parties irrevocably agree that any dispute arising out of or in connection with this License will be subject to and within the jurisdiction of the courts of {*jurisdiction*}.]

AS WITNESS the hands of the duly authorized representatives of the parties the day and year below first written

FOR THE PUBLISHER: [FULL NAME]

Name (in block capitals): _____ Date: _____

Position/Title: _____

FOR THE LICENSEE: [FULL NAME]

Name (in block capitals): _____ Date: _____

Position/Title: _____

SCHEDULE 1

LICENSED MATERIALS SUBSCRIPTION PERIOD AND ACCESS METHOD

A schedule dated [date] to the License dated [date] between [Publisher] and [Licensee]

THE LICENSED MATERIALS

Title	Subscription Period	Format	Delivery Schedule	Fee

List of Licensed Material, for each item list title, initial Subscription Period, including where relevant the start date and end date, format, delivery schedule (if applicable) and Fee for the initial Subscription Period. If back files are provided free of charge as part of the License, these should be listed specifically.

ACCESS METHOD

☐ Authentication via User ID/password and IP Address
☐ Authentication via IP address
☐ Authentication via Athens / Shibboleth: _____

AS WITNESS the hands of the duly authorized representatives of the parties the day and year below first written

FOR THE PUBLISHER: [FULL NAME]

Name (in block capitals): _____ Date: _____

Position/Title: _____

FOR THE LICENSEE: [FULL NAME]

Name (in block capitals): _____ Date: _____

Position/Title: _____

SCHEDULE 2

LIBRARY PREMISES

A schedule dated [date] to the License dated [date] between [Publisher] and [Licensee]

List of addresses of the Licensee's Library Premises, Domain Name(s) and IP addresses and/or ranges:
Class B Network: first two network numbers plus asterisks for host addresses, i.e.: 125.64.*.*
Class C network: first three network numbers plus an asterisk for host address, .i.e.: 125.64.133.*
Single station: all four numbers, i.e., 125.64.133.20; or ranges, i,e,. 125.64.133.20125 .64.133.40

Library name & address   Domain name(s)   Format   IP addresses/ranges

Network contact: Name:

Telephone: Fax: E-mail address:

AS WITNESS the hands of the duly authorized representatives of the parties the day and year below first written

FOR THE PUBLISHER: [FULL NAME]

Name (in block capitals): _____ Date: _____

Position/Title: _____

FOR THE LICENSEE: [FULL NAME]

Name (in block capitals): _____ Date: _____

Position/Title: _____

Appendix C

ARL Principles for Licensing Electronic Resources

(from: http://www.arl.org/sc/marketplace/license/licprinciples.shtml)
Principles for Licensing Electronic Resources (July '97)
Final Draft
July 15, 1997
American Association of Law Libraries
American Library Association
Association of Academic Health Sciences Libraries
Association of Research Libraries
Medical Library Association
Special Libraries Association

Introduction

License agreements are a fact of life in conducting business in the electronic environment. Providers of electronic information resources are employing licenses as a legal means of controlling the use of their products. In the electronic environment where the traditional print practice of ownership through purchase is being replaced by access through license, libraries need to be aware that licensing arrangements may restrict their legal rights and those of their users. As responsible agents for an institution, librarians must negotiate licenses that address the institution's needs and recognize its obligations to the licensor.

To help provide guidance in this continuously evolving environment, the American Association of Law Libraries, American Library Association, Association of Academic Health Sciences Libraries, Association of Research Libraries, Medical Library Association, and Special Libraries Association have combined to develop a statement of principles. These six associations represent an international membership of libraries of all types and sizes. The intent of this document is two-fold: to guide libraries in negotiating license agreements for access to electronic resources, and to provide licensors with a sense of the issues of importance to libraries and their user communities in such negotiations.

The Special Libraries Association provided funding to support the development and distribution of the principles.

Legal Background

A license agreement is a legal contract—"a promise or set of promises constituting an agreement between the parties that gives each a legal duty to the other and also the right to seek a remedy for the breach of those duties. Its essentials are competent parties, subject matter, a legal consideration, mutuality of agreement, and mutuality of obligations." [Black's Law Dictionary, 6th edition, 1990, p. 322.] Key to the concept of a contract is the fact that it is an agreement, a mutually acceptable set of understandings and commitments often arrived at through discussion and negotiation. Most commercial contracts are intended to spell out the mutual understandings between buyer and seller for products or services.

Although the original contract document may be the work product of either the buyer or seller, in a licensing situation, it is generally the seller (or licensor) who has prepared the agreement. It is imperative that the buyer (or licensee) review the terms of the agreement and communicate concerns to the licensor before signing it. Discussion may continue until either agreement is reached or a decision is made not to contract for the particular product or service. In the area of licensing electronic resources, failure to read and understand the terms of the agreement may result in such unintended consequences as:

the loss of certain rights to uses of the resource that would otherwise be allowed under the law (for example, in the United States, such uses as fair use, interlibrary loan, and other library and educational uses);

obligations to implement restrictions that are unduly burdensome or create legal risk for the institution; or,

sudden termination of the contract due to inappropriate use by a member of the user community.

Given the obligations that a contract creates for an institution and the possible liability associated with not meeting those obligations, most institutions will delegate the authority to sign contracts to a specific office or officer within the institution. In many institutions, this signatory authority will reside in the purchasing department, legal counsel's or vice president's office, or the library director's office, although in some institutions, a library staff member may be granted authority for signing license agreements. Nevertheless, library staff will often be responsible for initial review and negotiation of the material terms of the license because they have the most knowledge of the user community and of the resource being acquired. Library staff should be well informed of the uses critical to the library's user community (for example, printing, downloading, and copying).

An important category of license agreements is that including "shrink wrap" and "click" licenses. Such licenses are commonly found on the packaging of software, appear when software is loaded, or appear, sometimes buried, on Web sites. The terms of these licenses are made known to the user at the time the product is purchased, or just before or during use. The user has only two options: accept the license terms or do not use the software, electronic product, or Web site.

Traditional contract terminology defines these agreements as "contracts of adhesion," because there are no formal negotiations between licensor and licensee. Hence, the rules of use are imposed by one side, rather than evolved through a discussion leading to a mutual understanding or "meeting of the minds." While many courts reject these contracts or rewrite particular terms on the basis of equity, one cannot assume that the terms are unenforceable. In fact, some states are in the process of passing legislation that makes shrink wrap or click licenses enforceable. A purchasing library should consider contacting the licensor directly to determine if there are any license terms which can be modified to fit the special needs of libraries. Often, if there are competing products which can satisfy the user's needs equally well, exceptions to the form agreement may be negotiated. If negotiation is not possible, it is suggested that legal counsel be consulted for an opinion of enforceability prior to accepting or rejecting the product.

The following principles are meant to provide guidance to library staff in working with others in the institution and with licensors to create agreements that respect the rights and obligations of both parties.

Principles for Licensing Electronic Resources

1. A license agreement should state clearly what access rights are being acquired by the licensee—permanent use of the content or access rights only for a defined period of time.
2. A license agreement should recognize and not restrict or abrogate the rights of the licensee or its user community permitted under copyright law. The licensee should make clear to the licensor those uses critical to its particular users including, but not limited to, printing, downloading, and copying.
3. A license agreement should recognize the intellectual property rights of both the licensee and the licensor.
4. A license agreement should not hold the licensee liable for unauthorized uses of the licensed resource by its users, as long as the licensee has implemented reasonable and appropriate methods to notify its user community of use restrictions.
5. The licensee should be willing to undertake reasonable and appropriate methods to enforce the terms of access to a licensed resource.
6. A license agreement should fairly recognize those access enforcement obligations which the licensee is able to implement without unreasonable burden. Enforcement must not violate the privacy and confidentiality of authorized users.
7. The licensee should be responsible for establishing policies that create an environment in which authorized users make appropriate use of licensed resources and for carrying out due process when it appears that a use may violate the agreement.
8. A license agreement should require the licensor to give the licensee notice of any suspected or alleged license violations that come to the attention of the licensor and allow a reasonable time for the licensee to investigate and take corrective action, if appropriate.

9. A license agreement should not require the use of an authentication system that is a barrier to access by authorized users.

10. When permanent use of a resource has been licensed, a license agreement should allow the licensee to copy data for the purposes of preservation and/or the creation of a usable archival copy. If a license agreement does not permit the licensee to make a usable preservation copy, a license agreement should specify who has permanent archival responsibility for the resource and under what conditions the licensee may access or refer users to the archival copy.

11. The terms of a license should be considered fixed at the time the license is signed by both parties. If the terms are subject to change (for example, scope of coverage or method of access), the agreement should require the licensor or licensee to notify the other party in a timely and reasonable fashion of any such changes before they are implemented, and permit either party to terminate the agreement if the changes are not acceptable.

12. A license agreement should require the licensor to defend, indemnify, and hold the licensee harmless from any action based on a claim that use of the resource in accordance with the license infringes any patent, copyright, trade-mark, or trade secret of any third party.

13. The routine collection of use data by either party to a license agreement should be predicated upon disclosure of such collection activities to the other party and must respect laws and institutional policies regarding confidentiality and privacy.

14. A license agreement should not require the licensee to adhere to unspecified terms in a separate agreement between the licensor and a third party unless the terms are fully reiterated in the current license or fully disclosed and agreed to by the licensee.

15. A license agreement should provide termination rights that are appropriate to each party.

APPENDICES

A. Terms to be Defined by the Licensee Within a License Agreement

A license agreement should define clearly the terms used and should use those terms consistently throughout. The licensee should take responsibility for defining the following terms appropriate to its user community:

archive authorized use authorized user concurrent use institution local access local area network remote access simultaneous use site wide area network

B. Resources on Licensing

Brennan, Patricia, Karen Hersey, and Georgia Harper. Licensing Electronic Resources: Strategic and Practical Considerations for Signing Electronic Information Delivery Agreements. Washington: Association of Research Libraries, 1997. Also on the Web http://www.arl.org/sc/marketplace/license/licbooklet.shtml.

"LibLicense: Licensing Electronic Resources." Website and Discussion List. 1996. http://www.library.yale.edu/~llicense/index.shtml.

University of Texas System Contains a range of resources related to copyright in the library. Includes an interactive Software and Database License Agreement Checklist. http://www.utsystem.edu/ogc/intellectualproperty/cprtindx.htm.

C. Sources Consulted

The Working Group would like to thank a number of individuals and organizations for sharing with us drafts, notes, and memos about licensing principles that are not publicly available: Trisha Davis and Brian Schottlaender, the Association of Academic Health Sciences Libraries, Massachusetts Institute of Technology, and the University of New Mexico. Other sources the Working Group consulted are listed below. We would also like to thank the many individuals—librarians, vendors, publishers, and lawyers—who reviewed earlier drafts and provided excellent feedback, and the Special Libraries Association for providing the funding for this effort.

American Library Association, Association for Library Collections & Technical Services, Publisher/Vendor Library Relations Committee, Electronic Publishing Licensing Agreements Subcommittee. "Guidelines Document, Draft 2.2." 20 June 1995.

Brennan, Patricia, Karen Hersey, and Georgia Harper. Licensing Electronic Resources: Strategic and Practical Considerations for Signing Electronic Information Delivery Agreements. Washington: Association of Research Libraries, 1997. Also on the Web http://www.arl.org/sc/marketplace/license/licbooklet.shtml.

California State University Libraries. "CSU Principles for Acquisition of Electronic Information Resources (Draft)." 9 Jan. 1997.

Coalition for Networked Information.

"Draft Preliminary Findings of the Rights for Electronic Access to and Delivery of Information (READI) Project." Prepared by Robert Ubell Associates. http://www.cni.org/projects/READI/draft-rpt/, 3 Sept. 1996.

European Copyright User Platform. "Heads of Agreement for Site-Licenses for the Use of Electronic Publications." 25 Sept. 1996.

———. "Position on User Rights in Electronic Publications." 25 Sept. 1996.

Ferguson, Tony. "I Am Beginning to Hate Commercial E-Journals." Against the Grain. Sept. 1996: 86.

Hersey, Karen. "Coping with Copyright and Beyond: New Challenges as the Library Goes Digital." Copyright, Public Policy, and the Scholarly Community. Washington: Association of Research Libraries, 1995. 23–32.

Jacobson, Robert L. "Colleges Urged to Protect Rights in Licensing Negotiations." Chronicle of Higher Education. 5 July 1996: A15.

"LibLicense: Licensing Electronic Resources." Website and Discussion List. 1996. http://www.library.yale.edu/~Llicense/index.shtml.

National Humanities Alliance. "Basic Principles for Managing Intellectual Property in the Digital Environment." 24 Mar. 1997.

University of California Libraries, Collection Development Committee. "Principles for Acquiring and Licensing Information in Digital Formats." 22 May 1996. http://libraries.universityofcalifornia.edu/cdc/principlesforacquiring.html, 22 Oct. 1996.

Warro, Edward A. "What Have We Been Signing? A Look at Database Licensing Agreements." Library Administration and Management 8.3 (1994): 173–177.

Members of the Working Group

American Association of Law Libraries, Robert Oakley

American Library Association, Trisha Davis

American Library Association, Association for Library Collections & Technical Services, Collection Management and Development Section, Chief Collection Development Officers of Large Research Libraries, Brian Schottlaender

Association of Academic Health Sciences Libraries, Karen Butter

Association of Research Libraries, Mary Case

Medical Library Association, Karen Butter

Special Libraries Association, John Latham

The members of the Working Group welcome your comments on this document.

Appendix D

Sample Problem Scenarios

(adapted from the Tech Problem Log at _____ College Library)

Choose Any Three

Problem Report #1:
Info: Biography Database and Business Database are both from Vendor X.

----- Original Message -----
Date Submitted: 10/23/07 11:08
A new Problem has been submitted by *Reference Librarian A*
Problem: biography database is not connecting, 2 pm Tuesday

----- First Response to Original Message -----
On Oct 23, 2007, at 2:22 PM, Karin Wikoff wrote:
From where? Send me some details. I just tried it and got in fine.

----- Response to First Response to Original Message -----
I just tried again & got in ok. I asked Reference Librarian B to
check & he couldn't get in either. Then I went to Business Database & it was glitchy, too. – Reference Librarian A

Problem Report #2:
----- Original Message -----
Journal Collection Y. Cite: Modern Asian Studies, 23(2) 1989.
Class needs to access. Can not access via search, only by browsing
(!) http://www.journalcollectiony.org/stable/i213782 (seems
to be a glitch specific to this article). Reference Librarian A
(passed on by Reference Librarian C)

Problem Report #3:

----- Original Message -----
The Vendor O software license is exceeded. All user licenses are currently in use. Please try again later. I received this message at 9 am Monday morning. Please check. Seems like an odd message for 9 am.

Problem Report #4:

----- Original Message -----
Streaming Music Collection Z does not seem to be recognizing our IP address. Using either Firefox or IE, patrons are prompted to enter username/password.

Problem Report #5:

----- Original Message -----
Database H: cannot search on my desk computer. Reference Librarian D tried it on the Ref desk and it works fine. Application Error * DatabaseH® is not able to process your request at this time. Please try again later. If you continue to experience difficulties, please contact your customer service representative.

Problem Report #6:

Info: Financial Database Q access is via IP address, not id/pwd.
----- Original Message -----
Financial Database Q. It connects to an email / password screen. I've not used this yet. Is that correct?

Problem Report #7:

----- Original Message -----
Subscription E-book Collection: All text pages are reporting "The requested page could not be accessed on the server. It may be available at a smaller zoom." They do not display at any zoom.

[After writing up your strategies for solving these issues, see APPENDIX G: SAMPLE PROBLEM SCENARIOS: STRATEGIES AND OUTCOMES for suggestions and outcomes of the real-life problems.]

Appendix E

Sample Evaluation

(from a form-generated e-mail to Karin Wikoff)

Date Submitted: March 29, 20—

Name: ——

Name of Product: LION (Literature Online)
Publisher/Vendor: ProQuest
Who will use the resource: undergrads, grad_students, faculty
Which department will likely use: English and Theatre
Will it require special training: Yes
Notes on training: There's so much functionality that training will be especially helpful for users.
What type of user support is available:
Notes on support:

Type and Breadth: full_text abstracts bib_citations
Type and Breadth—other:
Current size: 350,000 literary texts, 930,000 works of criticism
Dates of Coverage—Retrospective: The ABELL bibliography goes back to 1920
Dates of Coverage—Current range: Available full-text from ABELL is fairly recent, usually no earlier than about 1990, and on average kicking in around 1997.
How Unique:
Equivalent print resource already owned:
Equivalent e-resource already owned: If we bought this packaged with the MLA bib, it would replace both that and the Literature Resource Center.
Need for archival access:

Flat rate/unlimited access:
Flat rate for simultaneous users:
Flat rate per simultaneous user:
Based on FTE users:
Based on library holding of print resource:
Separate License cost:
Other costs:

Where does resource reside:
Other residence:

Hardware/software requirements:
What is required to access:
Other required to access:

Statistical reports available:
Access after cancellation:
Permission to locally archive:
Restrictions:

Well-designed search engine: agree
Sufficient access for users: agree
Overall easy to use: agree
Faithful to print original:
Potential of heavy use: agree
Intuitive interface: agree

General Comments: As I said above, there is so much functionality and so many different types of resources available here that I think navigation is sometimes a problem.
But if we bundle it with the MLA, it provides us with a better interface for that than
Gale does. The 350,000 literary works available are a mixed bag. Coverage is spotty,
and there is always the question of who would want to read longer works online (and
these longer works require massive downloads—and we should probably ask if this
has implications for the IC network). But it does provide Keyword searching of any
and all full-text, which would allow the pinpointing of words and phrases across an
author's available work. If, as Karin and I discussed, Lion + MLA actually would
represent a savings over Gale MLA + Lit. Resource Cent., then I suppose we should
go with LION.

Appendix F

Related Readings

BOOKS

Conger, Joan E. *Collaborative Electronic Resources Management: From Acquisitions to Assessment.* Westport, CT: Libraries Unlimited, 2004. [Section on License Negotiation]

Gregory, V. L. *Selecting and Managing Electronic Resources: A How-to-Do-It Manual for Librarians.* New York: Neal-Shuman, 2006.

Kovacs, Diane K., and Robinson, Kara L. *The Kovacs Guide to Electronic Library Collection Development: Essential Core Subject Collections, Selection Criteria, and Guidelines.* New York: Neal-Schuman, 2004.

ARTICLES

Bhatt, J., and Denick, D. (2009). JISC's Academic Database Assessment Tool as a Collection Development and Management Tool for Bibliographic Databases. *Collection Management, 34*(3), 234–41.

Blecic, D. D., Fiscella, J. B., and Wiberley, S. E., Jr. (2007). Measurement of Use of Electronic Resources: Advances in Use Statistics and Innovations in Resource Functionality. *College & Research Libraries, 68*(1), 26–44.

Botero, C., Carrico, S., and Tennant, M. (2008). Using Comparative Online Journal Usage Studies To Assess the Big Deal. *Library Resources & Technical Services, 52*(2), 61–68.

Brinley, F., and Plum, T. (2006). Successful Web Survey Methodologies for Measuring the Impact of Networked Electronic Services. *IFLA Journal, 32*(1), 28–40.

Brown, C. C., and Meagher, E. S. (2008) Cataloging Free E-Resources: Is It Worth the Investment? *Interlending & Document Supply, 36*(3), 135–41.

Brown-Sica, M. (2008). Playing Tag in the Dark: Diagnosing Slowness in Library Response Time. *Information Technology and Libraries, 27*(4), 29–32.

Chilton, G., Doering, W. (2009) ERMes: Open Source Simplicity for Your E-Resource Management. *Computers in Libraries, 29*(8) 20.

Chisman, J. (2008). Electronic Resource Usage Data: Standards and Possibilities. *The Serials Librarian, 53*, 79–89.

Chisman, J., Matthews, G., and Brady, C. (2007). Electronic Resource Management. *The Serials Librarian, 52*(3/4), 297–303.

Chudnov, D. (2009). Practical Geek-Keeping, or, How To Hire—and Keep—Good Technical Staff. *Computers in Libraries, 29*(1), 25–26.

Clark, C. (2009). Shifting Sands: The Changing Landscape of Managing Electronic Resources. *Louisiana Libraries, 71*(3), 19–20.

Cole, L. (2009). The E-Deal: Keeping Up to Date and Allowing Access to the End User. *The Serials Librarian, 57*(4), 399.

Collins, Maria. (2009). Evolving Workflows: Knowing When To Hold 'Em, Knowing When To Fold 'Em. *The Serials Librarian, 57*, 261–71.

Day, R., and Cernichiari, A. (2008). Evolving Concepts and Business Models for Acquiring Electronic Resources: An Agent and Publisher Perspective. *The Serials Librarian, 53*(4), 195–203.

Dehmlow, M. (2009). The Ten Commandments of Interacting with Nontechnical People. *Information Technology and Libraries, 28*(2), 53–54.

Deng, H. (2010). Emerging Patterns and Trends in Utilizing Electronic Resources in a Higher Education Environment: An Empirical Analysis. *New Library World, 111*(3/4), 87–103.

Dinkelman, A., and Stacy-Bates, K. (2007). Accessing E-Books Through Academic Library Web Sites. *College & Research Libraries, 68*(1), 45–58.

Donlan, Rebecca. (2008). Boulevard of Broken Links: Keeping Users Connected to E-Journal Content. *The Reference Librarian, 48*(1), 99–104.

Eggleston, H., and Ginanni, K. (2009). Simplifying Licensed Resource Access Through Shibboleth. *The Serials Librarian, 56*(1), 209–14.

Ellis, L. A., Hartnett, J., and Waldman, M. (2008). Building Bearcat. *Library Journal (1976) Net Connect*, 6–8.

Feather, C. (2007). Electronic Resources Communications Management: A Strategy for Success. *Library Resources & Technical Services, 51*(3), 204–11, 228.

Fenton, E. G. (2008). Responding to the Preservation Challenge: Portico, an Electronic Archiving Service. *Journal of Library Administration, 48*(1), 31–40.

Flatley, R., and Prock, K. (2009). E-Resource Collection Development: A Survey of Current Practices in Academic Libraries. *Library Philosophy and Practice, 2009*, 1–5.

Fortini, T. (2007). Going Online: Academic Libraries and the Move From Print to Electronic Journals. *Library Student Journal 2*(6), 3–11.

Fuller, K., Livingston, J., Brown, S. W., Cowan, S., Wood, T., and Porter, L. (2009). Making Unmediated Access To E-Resources a Reality: Creating a Usable ERM Interface. *Reference & User Services Quarterly, 48*(3), 287–301.

Grensing-Pophal, L. (2009). Social Media Helps Out the Help Desk. *EContent, 32*(9), 6–41.

Grogg, J. E., and Ashmore, B. (2009). The Art of the Deal: Negotiating in Times of Economic Stress. *Searcher 17*(6), 42–49.

Harcourt, M. W., and Wolley, I. (2007). Automated Access Level Cataloging for Internet Resources at Columbia University Libraries. *Library Resources & Technical Services 51*(3), 212–25.

Hightower, B., Rawl, C., and Schutt, M. (2008). Collaborations for Delivering the Library to Students through WebCT. *Reference Services Review 35*(4), 541–51.

Hulseberg, A., and Monson, S. (2009) Strategic Planning for Electronic Resources Management: A Case Study at Gustavus Adolphus College, *Journal of Electronic Resources Librarianship, 21*(2), 163–71.

Jacso, P. (2009). Database Source Coverage: Hypes, Vital Signs and Reality Checks. *Online Information Review 33*(5), 997–1007.

Lawrence, P. (2009). Access When and Where They Want It: Using Ezproxy to Serve Our Remote Users. *Computers in Libraries, 29*(1), 6–7, 41–43.

Linberger, P., Fielding, L. J., and Bove, F. J. (2007). Developing a Web-Based Evaluation Tool for Purchasing Electronic Resources: A Librarian-Faculty-Student Partnership. *Electronic Journal of Academic and Special Librarianship*, 8(3), 17.

Liu, G. (2009). ERM System Implementation in a Consortium Environment. *Library Management, 30*(1/2), 35–43.

Llona, E., Craft, E., Yakota-Carter, K., and Pham, D. (2004). Providing Access to Foreign Language Electronic Resources. *Foreign Language Electronic Resources, 23*(3), 119.

Makri, S., Blandford, A., and Cox, A. (2008). Using Information Behaviors to Evaluate the Functionality and Usability of Electronic Resources: From Ellis' Model to Evaluation. *Journal of the American Society for Information Science and Technology 59*(14), 2244–67.

McCracken, P., and Arthur, M. A. (2009). KBART: Best Practices in Knowledgebase Data Transfer. *The Serials Librarian 56*(1), 230–35.

McElfresh, L. (2008). Standing at the Edge of ERMS. *Technicalities, 28*(1), 3–5.

Miller, R. (2008). Acts of Vision: The Practice of Licensing. *Collection Management, 32*(1/2), 173–90.

Mitchell, N., and Lorbeer, E. R. (2009). Building Relevant and Sustainable Collections. *The Serials Librarian, 57*(4), 327–33.

Morrisey, L. (2010). Data-Driven Decision Making in Electronic Collection Development. *Journal of Library Administration, 50*(30), 283–90.

Negrucci, T. (2008). E-Usage Data: The Basics. *Colorado Library 34*(1), 48–50.

Noh, Y. (2010). A Study on Developing Evaluation Criteria for Electronic Resources in Evaluation Indicators of Libraries, *Journal of Academic Librarianship, 36*(1), 41–52.

O'Hara, L. H. (2007). Providing Access to Electronic Journals in Academic Libraries. *The Serials Librarian, 51*(3), 119–28.

Paynter, Robin A. (2009). Commercial Library Decision Support Systems: An Analysis Based on Collection Managers' Needs. *Collection Management, 34*(1), 31–47.

Price, A. (2009). How to Make a Dollar Out of Fifteen Cents: Tips for Electronic Collection Development. *Collection Building* (28), 31–34.

Resnick T., and Clark, D. (2009). Evolution of Electronic Resources Support: Is Virtual Reference the Answer? *Library Hi Tech*, 27(3), 357–71.

Resnick, T., Ugaz, A., Buford, N., and Carrigan, E. (2008). E-resources: Transforming Access Services for the Digital Age. *Library Hi Tech 26*(1), 141–56.

Rolnik, Z., Lamoureux, S., and Smith, K. A. (2008). Alternatives to Licensing of E-Resources. *The Serials Librarian 54*(3), 281–87.

Ruth, L., and Collins, M. (2008). License Mapping for ERM Systems: Existing Practices and Initiatives for Support. *Serials Review, 34*(2), 137–43.

Sanville, T. (2008). Do Economic Factors Really Matter in the Assessment and Retention of Electronic Resources Licensed at the Library Consortium Level? *Collection Management, 33*(1), 1–16.

Skaggs, B. L., Poe, J. W., and Stevens, K. W. (2006). One-Stop Shopping: A Perspective on the Evolution of Electronic Resources Management. *International Digital Library Perspectives, 22*(3) 192–206.

Stemper, J., and Barribeau, S. (2006). Perpetual Access to Electronic Journals: A Survey of One Academic Research Library's Licenses. *Library Resources & Technical Services, 50*(2), 91–109.

Strader, C. R., Roth, A. C., and Boissy, R. W. (2008). E-Journal Access: A Collaborative Checklist for Libraries, Subscription Agents, and Publishers. *The Serials Librarian 55*(1), 98–116.

Tank, E., and Frederiksen, C. (2007). The Daisy Standard: Entering the Global Virtual Library. *Library Trends, 55*(4), 932–49.

Tenopir, C. (2010). E-Access Changes Everything. *Library Journal, 135*(1), 26.

Tonkery, Dan (2009) Publishers, Agents, Users, and Libraries: Coming of Age in the E-World, *The Serials Librarian, 57*(3), 253–60.

Vignau, B. S. S., and Quesada, R. L. P. (2006). Collection Development in a Digital Environment: An Imperative for Information Organizations in the Twenty-first Century. *Collection Building, 25*(4), 139–44.

Webster, Peter (2006). Bit by Bit, *netConnect, 0.2006(2006),* 16.

Whittaker, M. (2008). The Challenge of Acquisitions in the Digital Age. *Portal: Libraries and the Academy, 8*(4), 439–45.

Yi, H., and Herlihy, C. S.(2007). Assessment of the Impact of an Open-URL Link Resolver. *New Library World, 108*(7/8), 317–31.

Yue, P. W. and Anderson, R. (2007). Capturing Electronic Journals Management in a Flowchart. *The Serials Librarian, 51*(3), 101–18.

Appendix G

Sample Problem Scenarios: Strategies And Outcomes

Problem Report #1: Vendor X Biography Database and Business Database: Strategies/Outcome:

Because multiple users have tried and had trouble, we can posit that the problem isn't with the user's machine. You may want to check with your ITS department to see if there are known sporadic network problems, or you may want to start with the vendor, which is what I did. That led to the answer—Vendor X had had a brief outage the previous day that had caused some trouble but it had since been corrected, and we saw no more trouble.

Problem Report #2: Journal Collection Y Modern Asian Studies Article: Strategies/Outcome:

Your best clue here is that you *can* get to the article via browsing. Your first test, after reproducing the problem yourself, might be to try to search for some other article using indexing. If that works, and it did, there is a problem with the indexing. That was the case. We notified Journal Collection Y, and they put it on their list to correct the problem, and in the meanwhile, we sent a copy of the article to the faculty member via e-mail (or you could provide instructions for the alternate access method via browsing).

Problem Report #3: Vendor O License Exceeded Error Message: Strategies/Outcome:

First thing here is to make sure your bill has been paid! Check the license, too. Do you have limited simultaneous users, and if so, how many? In this case, we had dropped our online subscription and no longer had access to the particular title at all, but had not yet removed links from our Serials Solutions profile. The error message was misleading, which happens sometimes.

Problem Report #4: Streaming Music Collection Z Prompt for ID/Password: Strategies/Outcome:

To troubleshoot, try to reproduce the problem; also check from various browsers; call the vendor, then your local ITS. In this case, the problem was erratic, coming and going with no logical pattern discernible. This was the first sign of a big problem that took a lot of back and forth with a lot of people. It turned out to be a major change made by our ITS department to do load-balancing at the packet level. That means that for every packet sent with each and every different click of the mouse, the communication was dynamically assigned a different IP address, and they had added a whole additional new range we did not have registered with our several hundred vendors and publishers. So, any given click might get an IP in range and go through, while the next one might get an IP out of range and it would not go through. This led to an opportunity for ITS to learn more about how our resources work and how their decision impacted our work. It took months of tedious work contacting all our vendors to update our IP ranges.

Problem Report #5: Database H Application Error: Strategies/Outcome:

Because the user is having trouble on her computer but things are working fine from the reference desk right nearby, you might start by focusing on the user's computer. In this case, the user is on a Mac and the reference desk is on a PC. Test on other machines. We found the problem was sporadic, but most common on Macs. In the long run, it eventually was discovered to be a known yet intermittent problem that took Database H a long time to solve. Continued communication with the vendor and repeat testing with users was required over many months.

Problem Report #6: Financial Database Q Prompt for ID/Password: Strategies/Outcome:

When you are prompted for a password, it means the server at the other end is not recognizing you as an authorized user. So, check your IP address, check your proxy to make sure it is set up right, and check to be sure you've paid your bill. This vendor had forgotten to bill us, so we had not paid them, and they pulled the plug, also failing to notify us of that change either. We contacted them, got access turned right back on, and finally got the bill, although it meant we had to pay twice in one fiscal year for the same resource because we had passed our fiscal year end.

Problem Report #7: Subscription E-book Collection Inaccessible Page Error: Strategies/Outcome:

Try to reproduce the problem, if you can; check with the vendor. If you can't, check with the user. When did the problem occur? It was working again by the time I got to test it. Further investigation revealed that Subscription Ebook Collection had done some maintenance and we had not received the notice.

Appendix H

Sample Estimated Expenses Spreadsheet

Database	Vendor	06-07	%	Pd 07-08	%	Pd 08-09	%	Pd 09-10	%	Est. 10-11	Pd 10-11	%	NOTES
		$ 3,500.00	0%	$ 3,745.00	7%	$ 3,745.00	0%	$ 3,745.00	0%	$ 3,782.45	$ 3,745.00	1.0%	**Formerly called AP Photo Archive**
		$ 2,538.54	—	$ 2,940.00	16%	$ 2,756.25	-6%	$ 2,866.50	4%	$ 3,009.83	$ 2,866.50	5.0%	**5 mo. (08/09) from 1 Aug ($2,963.62) + 2009 ($7,450.80)**
		$ 6,897.24	6%	$ 7,112.70	3%	$ 10,414.42	46%	7,450.80	-28%	$ 8,121.37	$ 7,793.73	9.0%	
		$ 995.00	0%	$ 995.00	0%	$ 995.00	0%	$ 995.00	0%	$ 995.00	$ 995.00	0.0%	**Calendar year pymts; exp. date 25 March**
		$ 937.00	-82%	$ 977.00	4%	$ 1,019.00	4%	$ 1,019.00	0%	$ 1,039.38	$ 1,044.00	2.0%	**Calendar year pymts; 06–07 due to reduced subscriptions**
		$ 8,500.00	-29%	$ 8,500.00	0%	$ 8,800.00	4%	$ 9,020.00	3%	$ 9,245.00	$ 9,245.00	2.5%	**Calendar year pymts; Pro-rated, one-time fee, but no annual fee for 04; half-year fee for '05 discounted 20% from $4,250 (05–06: $3,400=$8,500=$11,900)**
		$ 9,614.91	7%	$ 11,311.65	18%	$ 5,655.82	-50%	$ 5,797.67	3%	$ 6,000.59	$ 5,797.67	3.5%	**Pro-rated for 04–05**
		$ 1,863.95	—	$ –	—	$ 1,491.16	—	$ 1,491.16	0%	$ 1,520.98	$ 1,940.04	2.0%	**14 months with 2 free pd 06–07 through 07–08; 5SU**
		$ –	—	$ 2,244.38	7%	$ 2,244.38	0%	$ 2,244.38	0%	$ 2,289.27	$ 2,244.38	2.0%	**2-yr deal; pd in full 05–06; incl. admin fee; 3SU**
											$ 795.00		**New in July 2010**
											$ 3,498.00		**New in July 2010**
		$ 1,370.00	—	$ –	—	$ 1,294.12	—	$ 1,294.12	0%	$ 1,320.00	$ 1,294.12	2.0%	**Paid early 06–07 for 07–08**
		$ 2,403.12	10%	$ 2,485.51	3%	$ 2,592.38	4%	$ 2,396.89	-8%	$ 2,516.73	$ 2,727.22	5.0%	**Fewer FTE=lower price 09–10**
ETC		—	—	$ 1,698.75	0%	$ 1,798.75	6%	$ 100.00	-94%	$ 100.00	$ 100.00	0.0%	**Vendor failed to bill us before end of FY06/07; splitting fee 07/08 & 08/09; $100 access fee thereafter; $100 added 3/17/09**
		$ 320.00	0%	$ 320.00	0%	$ 320.00	0%	$ 320.00	0%	$ 320.00		0.0%	
								$ 38,740.52		$ 40,260.60			

Appendix I

Sample Statistics Spreadsheet

Database Name	YTD	June 10	May 10	Apr 10	Mar 10	Feb 10	Jan 10	Dec 09	Nov 09	Oct 09	Sep 10	Aug 09	July 09
ACS Journals	440	7	27	118	60	25	23	56	50	24	9	9	32
SciFinder Scholar	2,506	479	120	371	230	363	77	103	236	105	154	95	173
PsychiatryOnline	90	1	9	30	6	12	1	4	4	14	4	4	1
MathSci Net	698	88	114	15	40	28	72	74	63	59	63	17	65
Annual Reviews	197	4	20	70	39	18	5	6	8	4	23	0	0
ARTstor	45,935	1,029	3,269	6,543	3,986	4,680	4,022	4,154	6,773	4,509	4,681	2,121	168
KCDLonline	38	1	4	4	1	2	2	3	5	7	6	1	2
Britannica Online	1,811	60	172	265	147	137	36	256	409	173	107	10	39
LION (Literature Online) with MLA	2,457	74	399	248	142	148	80	351	464	138	196	99	118
MLA Intl Bibliography on PQ/Chadwyck-Healey	1,999	60	179	236	227	176	111	153	350	181	147	78	101
MPAO (IIMP)	2,015	12	65	178	158	170	18	81	180	363	177	126	487
CQ Electronic Library	19	0	2	8	3	1	0	5	0	0	0	0	0
ETC													
Total	58,205	1,815	4,380	8,086	5,039	5,760	4,447	5,246	8,542	5,577	5,567	2,560	1,186

Appendix J

Sample Cost-Per-Use Spreadsheet

Database	Vendor	Pd 09–10	Searches	$ per search
		$ 2,016.00	36,757	$ 0.05
		$ 3,395.46	42,864	$ 0.08
		$ 3,719.10	24,753	$ 0.15
		$ 9,020.00	45,935	$ 0.20
		$ 542.93	2,752	$ 0.20
		$ 1,488.27	7,446	$ 0.20
		$ 8,372.52	24,698	$ 0.34
		$ 7,615.77	22,173	$ 0.34
		$ 1,766.74	5,108	$ 0.35
		$ 20,300.00	58,653	$ 0.35
		$ 11,355.12	31,961	$ 0.36
		$ 2,568.25	7,156	$ 0.36
		$ 2,195.04	5,455	$ 0.40
		$ 12,555.62	30,563	$ 0.41
		$ 2,005.00	4,327	$ 0.46
		$ 320.00	571	$ 0.56
		$ 420.00	581	$ 0.72
		$ 4,977.18	6,084	$ 0.82
		$ 37,633.12	43,063	$ 0.87
		$ 5,047.82	5,076	$ 0.99
		$ 2,396.89	1,811	$ 1.32
		$ 8,167.41	6,036	$ 1.35
		$ 9,303.83	4,185	$ 2.22
		$ 2,600.00	1,065	$ 2.44
		$ 17,190.00	4,796	$ 3.58
		$ 7,730.10	2,037	$ 3.79
		$10,814.84	2,575	$ 4.20
		$ 11,766.41	2,457	$ 4.79
		$ 1,019.00	197	$ 5.17
		$ 1,710.71	317	$ 5.40
		$157,334.25	23,652	$ 6.65
		$ 790.13	112	$ 7.05
		$ 6,742.01	903	$ 7.47
		$7,450.80	698	$ 10.67
		$ 1,656.56	69	$ 24.01
		$ 2,866.50	90	$ 31.85
		$ 1,294.12	38	$ 34.06

Appendix K

Sample Syllabus

School of Information Studies
IST 502 New Directions in Academic Libraries
2009–2010

NOTES ON THIS SYLLABUS: This is a draft of a developing course. Dates and assignments may change, but ample warning will be given.

> **Instructor contact information and office hours:**
> **Karin Wikoff**
> Email address
> W: Work Phone number
> H: Home Phone number
> Mailing Address: Home address
> I am usually at work from 7:15 AM to 3:15 PM. I have voice mail at both home and work and will respond as soon as I can. I will be sure to be available at home Tuesdays from 5–6 PM ET and at work Thursdays from 11AM–12N ET.

Course Description:

Licensed electronic resources have become the cornerstone of academic research, making the management of these resources mission-critical for college and university libraries. This course will cover the whole life cycle of electronic resources, from acquiring through providing access, administering, supporting, and evaluating. Specific issues will include: vendor relations, negotiating contracts, access models, troubleshooting, gathering and using statistics, collection development, linking technologies, and much more. We will also touch briefly on information commons and institutional archives. At the end of the course, students should have a grasp of the issues they would face as an electronic resources librarian along with some practical working knowledge to get them started in this exciting and fast-paced field.

Pre- and/or Co-requisites: None

Learning objectives/learning outcomes

a. Learning Objective: What will you teach them? The basic issues of electronic resources management.

b. Learning Outcome: What will they be able to do? Take a job as an electronic resources librarian with enough of a grasp of these issues and enough practical knowledge to get started.

Texts (required and recommended), readings and supplies:

Required: Access to SU's electronic resources: In lieu of a textbook, each week, each student will locate and read an academic article on the current week's topic. Articles should be no more than 3 years old. Students will then write a 1–2 paragraph summary of each article, being sure to include the author's thesis, the author's conclusion, and their own reactions to the article. The summaries should be turned in by 5 PM ET each Friday (adjustments will be made for holidays and breaks). The instructor will select 1–2 articles from those submitted weekly by students for the whole class to read and discuss.

Recommended but not required: Selecting and Managing Electronic Resources: A How-To-Do-It Manual for Librarians. Vicki L. Gregory. Neal-Shuman, 2006.

Assignments and weights

Assignments:

A. The term project for this course will be to develop your own electronic resources collection development policy. This assignment will build on lessons learned through the course of the semester, both in class and from the students' own work outside class. Students will work on the project as teams of three, or as practical depending on the total number enrolled.

B. I will post a lecture and/or discussion starter every Monday. If I have it ready before Monday, I may post it sooner, but students will have content to read and upon which to comment by Monday at the latest every week we have class.

C. As noted previously, each student will be expected to contribute 1 article on specific topics each week, as well as reading the 2 articles selected by the instructor from the previous week. Discussion of these is part of the participation grade.

D. There will be 7 topic-based assignments, roughly every other week. These will involve some outside work and a short report or paper, as outlined in the individual assignments. The purpose of these assignments is to give you some contact and experience with real-world situations and to get you thinking about how you would handle them.

Weights:

35% of your grade will be based on your 7 **topic-based assignments**. Each assignment will be worth 5% of the final grade.

24% of your grade will be based on the submission of **two articles** weekly for 11 weeks, plus one term project update. That's 2% per assignment, with the same amount given to each member of the team for the term project portion.

21% of your grade will be based on your active engagement in online discussion of the weekly lectures, readings, and discussion starters. That's 14 weeks of discussion, each worth 1.5% of your final grade. It may not seem like much, but it adds up. This is where I expect a large portion of your learning to occur, so I cannot urge you strongly enough to keep up the meaningful **participation**.

20% of your grade will be based on the **collection development term project**. This is a team project, so every member of the team will receive the same grade for the project. Don't let your teammates down.

Instructor expectations

c. **Attendance**: Each student needs to "attend" the virtual online classroom space regularly, several times a week.

d. **Participation**: Very important. I expect the largest share of teaching and learning to go on in the lecture/discussion/interaction portion of the course, so this will count for a major part of the grade.

e. **Late assignments**: If a student knows ahead of time that there is a problem that will cause an assignment to be late, s/he may contact the instructor and make arrangements in advance. Decisions to accept late work will be on a case-by-case basis with no guarantee of acceptance if arrangements for a reasonable excuse made in advance.

f. **Grading scale**

g. **Group projects**: Group projects will receive one grade for all, so it will be up to the group to make sure each peer does his or her part. It is simply not possible for the instructor to pick apart who is responsible for what portion or share of a group project.

Required and recommended statements

Academic Integrity

The academic community of Syracuse University and of the School of Information Studies requires the highest standards of professional ethics and personal integrity from all members of the community. Violations of these standards are violations of a mutual obligation characterized by trust, honesty, and personal honor. As a community, we commit ourselves to standards of academic conduct, impose sanctions against those who violate these standards, and keep appropriate records of violations.

The Academic Integrity statement can be found at: http://supolicies.syr.edu/ethics/acad_integrity.htm

Students with Disabilities

In compliance with section 504 of the Americans with Disabilities Act (ADA), Syracuse University is committed to ensure that "no otherwise qualified individual with a disability . . . shall, solely by reason of disability, be excluded from participation in, be denied the benefits of, or be subjected to discrimination under any program or activity. . . ." If you feel that you are a student who may need academic accommodations due to a disability, you should immediately register with the Office of Disability Services (ODS) at 804 University Avenue, Room 308 3rd Floor, 315.443.4498 or 315.443.1371 (TTD only). ODS is the Syracuse University office that authorizes special accommodations for students with disabilities.

iSchool's Learning Management System (LMS)

The iSchool's learning management course tool is Blackboard Learning System CE (used to be called WebCT6). This learning management course tool (LMS) is used to facilitate distance learning and enhance main campus courses at the iSchool. It is a flexible, integrated environment where students can integrate course experiences into the real-world communities of work and play. The environment is composed of a number of elements that will help you be successful in both your current coursework and your lifelong learning opportunities.

Note: The iSchool uses its own version of Blackboard. We are not affiliated with the SU campus-wide Blackboard Enterprise System.

Here is the direct URL to bookmark your access to the iSchool's learning management system (LMS): http://ischool.syr.edu/learn. *Questions regarding the LMS should be directed to ilms@syr.edu or Peggy Brown at 315-443-9370.*

Ownership of Student Work

In compliance with the federal Family Educational Rights and Privacy Act, works in all media produced by students as part of their course participation at Syracuse University may be used for educational purposes, ***provided that the course syllabus makes clear that such use may occur***. It is understood that registration for and continued enrollment in a course where such use of student works is announced constitute permission by the student.

After such a course has been completed, any further use of student works will meet one of the following conditions: (1) the work will be rendered anonymous through the removal of all personal identification of the work's creator/originator(s); or (2) the creator/originator(s') written permission will be secured.

As a generally accepted practice, honors theses, graduate theses, graduate research projects, dissertations, or other exit projects submitted in partial fulfillment of degree requirements are placed in the Library, University Archives, or academic departments for public reference.

The Ownership of Student Work statement can be found at http://undergraduate studies.syr.edu/vc_faculty_letter2007.pdf.

Course calendar with due dates

This schedule is not yet fixed, and may well change before class begins.

January 18: MLK Day Holiday
January 19–24

Define four types of Resources:

> Databases
> E-Journals
> E-Books
> Services (Linking Technologies and Federated Search)

January 22: ***Assignment One (Defining Resources)*** due by 5 PM ET
January 22: One article on the subject of Information/Learning Commons (ahead of the discussion week)
January 23–26: Plan to visit (in person or virtually, as feasible) an Information/Learning Commons site

January 25–31
Information/Learning Commons

January 27: One article on the subject of Acquiring Electronic Resources
January 29: *Assignment Two (Information/Learning Commons)* due by 5 PM ET

February 1–14
Acquire:

> Assessing needs; curriculum fit (Collection Development decisions)
> Budget (Most for your money; price per search; comparison shopping)
> Price (Compare, Negotiate, Wheel and deal, Vendors, consortial agents)
> License (Acceptable? Negotiable?)
> Trials (When? who gets to see them?)
> Evaluations (Features; Functionality)
> Order
> Pay

February 3: One article on a different subject within the general topic of Acquiring E-Resources
February 10: One article on the subject of Providing Access to Electronic Resources
February 12: *Assignment Three (Webinar and Feature Report)* due by 5 PM ET

February 15–February 28
Provide Access:

> IP Address vs. ID/Password/User Registration
> Proxy Support
> Catalog
> Portals/Access Lists
> Authentication
> URL Maintenance
> Relations with institutional information infrastructure and ITS

February 17: One article on a different subject within the general topic of Providing Access to E-Resources
February 24: One article on the subject of Administering Electronic Resources
February 26: *Assignment Four (Portal and ITS)* due by 5 PM ET

March 1–13
Administer:

> ID/Passwords (Where needed)
> Admin modules (id/passwords, URLs)
> Preferences (settings)
> Holdings Lists and ERAMS (E-Resource Access and Management Service)
> Access Restrictions (Users, locations, SUs, software)
> Claiming (Understanding the relationship between publishers, vendors, and libraries)
> Rights for Use

March 3: One article on a different subject within the general topic of Administering E-Res

March 10: One article on the subject of Providing Support to E-Res *OR* Progress Report/Draft of Collection Development Term Project

March 12: *Assignment Five (Licenses)* due by 5 PM ET

March 14–21 BREAK

March 22–April 4
Provide Support:

    Troubleshooting/Triage
    Contact Information
    Software Needs
    Hardware Needs
    Problem Logs

March 24: Whichever of the above you did not turn in before Spring Break

March 31: One article on the subject of Evaluating/Monitoring Electronic Resources

April 2: *Assignment Six (Troubleshooting)* due by 5 PM ET

April 5–18
Evaluate/Monitor:

    Review problems
    Downtime analysis
    Usage Stats; price per use
    User feedback

April 7: One article on a different subject within the general topic of Evaluating/Monitoring E-Res

April 14: One article on the subject of Institutional Archives, ahead of the discussion week

April 16: *Assignment Seven (Trials/Evaluation)* due by 5 PM ET

April 19–25
Institutional Archives

April 23: Request for discussion of subjects of interest not yet covered in curriculum

April 26–May 2

Collection Development policies

April 26: This week will be dedicated to working on the Collection Development Term Project

May 4: *Collection Development Term Project* due by 5 PM ET

Index

About the Author

KARIN WIKOFF is the Electronic and Technical Services Librarian at Ithaca College Library in Ithaca, NY, where she has managed electronic resources since 2004, and before that at Wells College in Aurora, NY. She has taught the management of electronic resources at Syracuse University's School of Information Studies and as a series of workshops through Nylink. She may be the only female librarian in the United States who is also a former professional football player.

Edwards Brothers, Inc.
Thorofare, NJ USA
November 21, 2011